Lifetimes

Exploring your past lives and life
between lives can empower you to
live the life you were meant to live

Marilyn Kaufman

BALBOA.PRESS
A DIVISION OF HAY HOUSE

Balboa Press books may be ordered through booksellers or by contacting:

Balboa Press
A Division of Hay House
1663 Liberty Drive
Bloomington, IN 47403
www.balboapress.com
844-682-1282

Because of the dynamic nature of the Internet, any web addresses or links contained in this book may have changed since publication and may no longer be valid. The views expressed in this work are solely those of the author and do not necessarily reflect the views of the publisher, and the publisher hereby disclaims any responsibility for them.

The author of this book does not dispense medical advice or prescribe the use of any technique as a form of treatment for physical, emotional, or medical problems without the advice of a physician, either directly or indirectly. The intent of the author is only to offer information of a general nature to help you in your quest for emotional and spiritual well-being. In the event you use any of the information in this book for yourself, which is your constitutional right, the author and the publisher assume no responsibility for your actions.

Any people depicted in stock imagery provided by Getty Images are models, and such images are being used for illustrative purposes only. Certain stock imagery © Getty Images.

Print information available on the last page.

ISBN: 978-1-9822-7424-5 (sc)
ISBN: 978-1-9822-7426-9 (hc)
ISBN: 978-1-9822-7425-2 (e)

Library of Congress Control Number: 2021918858

Balboa Press rev. date: 09/21/2021

I had always known that I would take this path,
but yesterday I did not know that it would be today.
　　—Narihira, Japanese poet and philosopher

For Sydney Love,
who was just too pure
to remain on this earth plane
for very long.
Until we meet again in spirit.

CONTENTS

Preface xi

Acknowledgements xiii

Section 1—The Beginning, If There Ever Really Was One

Chapter 1   The Push 1

Chapter 2   Why I Wrote This Book 5

Section 2—Past Life Learnings

Chapter 3   Past Life Regression 13

Chapter 4   My Process 23

Chapter 5   Karma 29

Chapter 6   Forgiveness 43

Section 3—Between-Life Learnings

Chapter 7   Between-Life Soul Regression 49

Chapter 8   Pre-Life Planning and Spiritual
            Contracts 55

Chapter 9   Soul Groups, Soul Evolution, Soul
            Mates and Twin Flames 65

Section 4—Otherworldly Learnings

Chapter 10   Other Times 75

Chapter 11   Other Worlds 85

Chapter 12   Channelling 95

Section 5—Final Note

My Prayer 111

Epilogue 113

About the Author 115

PREFACE

I hardly know how I got here, except that I was compelled. The synchronicity of events in my life just seemed to gain momentum more and more each day, and sometimes I felt as though I had to hold on to my hat and hang on for dear life. Events just unfolded before me as if by destiny, rather than by my decisions. I now know that when I am on the right path, when I am on purpose, the universe puts everything in place, and I just seem to go with the flow.

ACKNOWLEDGEMENTS

I would like to thank the many people who have remembered their past or between lifetimes with me. You have trusted me enough to share some of your most intimate stories, issues, questions and lifetimes. We have had many amazing conversations together. You have made my life so much richer.

Thank you to my many teachers who have opened my mind and expanded my Spirit. Thank you to Susan Zavadil from Aromas Naturally and Willow Den and to Kathy Upper creator of Spiritual Niagara (spiritualniagara.ca), who have opened so many doors for me. Special thanks to Dr Tracy Kennedy, who read the first draft of this book and offered much wise advice.

Thank you to my spirit guides for their considerable patience with me, for their wisdom and for always being there for me.

Thank you to my beautiful daughters, who taught me to love unconditionally. And thank you to my husband for his love, and even though he has a hard time believing everything in this book, he has constantly supported me in everything I do.

SECTION 1

The Beginning, If There Ever Really Was One

CHAPTER 1

The Push

SOMETIMES SPIRIT GIVES US A little whisper or nudge when it wants to direct us to a certain path—a path that we have planned for ourselves. Our purpose. And sometimes it gives us a giant push that we just can't ignore. Apparently, I needed a giant push!

As I worked my way through the chaotic rush-hour traffic in Toronto one cold winter night, little did I know I was on the way to getting it. A push that would lead me to live the life I was meant to live, a path I planned before I was born. I was headed to the Transformational Arts College, where I was studying energy healing. TAC is a metaphysical school that blocks out the business world that is Toronto and allows Spirit to thrive.

The class that evening was on energy psychology. Its purpose was to teach us how to alleviate the stress surrounding a particular issue we were facing by tapping the meridians on the sides of our hands together. We were to express our issue as a setup statement, worded in a specific way, and then rate the level of anxiety it caused us from one to ten. I rated my stress level at seven.

The issue I wanted to work on was that my three daughters all lived in other cities; one was studying at university in Ottawa, and the other two were living in Montreal. The youngest was modelling and was preparing to go to a convention in Las Vegas with a company I knew nothing about. I formed my statement regarding the stress I felt about them living in other cities and the fact that I didn't have enough involvement in their everyday lives, particularly the youngest with her modelling career.

While focusing on our statements and tapping the sides of our hands together at meridians located there, the level of our anxiety was supposed to decrease. However, I felt my level of anxiety increasing and mentioned this to the teacher. She told me that sometimes that happens and to just keep tapping.

After a few more minutes, I began to have trouble breathing and started to hyperventilate. I became hysterical and had no understanding as to why. I was helped onto a massage table so I could lie down. I was scared and angry—furious. I saw myself standing in front of a crowd, a mob, really, and they were angry as well. They were yelling at me to hand over my baby. Why would they take my baby? I begged them to take me instead; she is so innocent.

The teacher worked with me, but she was not a hypnotherapist and was not sure how to handle the situation. She did her best to calm me down while all the other students sent positive energy my way.

After I calmed down and began to breathe normally again, the teacher asked if this was a past life issue.

I went right back into it and started to cry, "My baby, my baby." I had glimpses of myself hiding in a house with my other two children. The mob had taken my youngest child from me and threatened that if I didn't stop practicing my gifts, they would take my other children as well. They took my baby and burned her in a fire. I was hysterical.

A girl in my class with psychic abilities drew the picture on page 4. They are the impressions of what she saw as I was experiencing the memories. It took a while, but my teacher did get me to calm down. This experience was very traumatic for me. I didn't understand what had just happened. I had never experienced past life memories before this. Until that evening, I didn't have any absolute beliefs in reincarnation and past lives, but I was open-minded. This spontaneous past life regression had certainly opened my eyes.

I continued studying energy psychology and worked through that past life. During another glimpse into that life, I realized that it took place in Düsseldorf, Germany, in the eighteenth or nineteenth century. The baby that was burned was the same Spirit as my youngest daughter. I saw myself being accused of being a witch and hanged from a tree by the same mob. I remember so clearly the visual of the trees going down as Spirit left my body and rose rapidly skyward. Apparently, I hadn't stopped practicing my gifts. As it turned out, one of my gifts was making a tea for women who wanted to terminate an unwanted pregnancy. To punish me for this, the mob took my baby and killed her. In a third session, I was asked to forgive the people for taking the lives of my daughter and myself to erase any karma created there. Note: this (and more) can all be done in one session during a past life regression.

I found it amazing that my concerns for my daughter in this life actually stemmed from the loss of control I had in a past life. What other lifetimes could be influencing my current life? I had to find out more.

CHAPTER 2

Why I Wrote This Book

Why write a book on uncovering past lives?
Because the benefits for personal empowerment,
healing and enlightenment are tremendous.

—Ted Andrews

THAT PUSH WAS THE BEGINNING of my exploration into reincarnation and past life regression. I decided that as soon as I finished my energy-healing courses, I would learn regression through hypnotherapy. I found many classes offering hypnosis in the Toronto area, but they all seemed very clinical, stop smoking or weight loss being the big money makers. This was not what I was looking for.

Then one day in 2008, I received two catalogues offering speakers and workshops of a spiritual nature. One was from Lily Dale, a quaint community of mediums in upstate New York. The other was from Fellowships of the Spirit, a spiritualist church and self-discovery centre next door to Lily Dale. I found the exact course I was looking for, Spiritual Hypnotherapy offered at Fellowships of the Spirit. The course was to be taught by Dick Sutphen (sadly, Dick crossed over in 2020) and consisted of 200 hours of study over a three-month period. It taught not only past life regression but also Spirit contact therapy. I enrolled immediately. On the days we had class, we booked rooms at the amazing guest homes of Lily Dale. It's a place you really should experience at least once in your life.

5

This class fascinated me. I learned and experienced so much. Since then, I have conducted hundreds of past life regressions. I love this work. I love to guide people into their past lives and then help them meet their Spirit guides. It makes me happy and has brought so much learning, understanding and inspiration into my life.

I wrote this book because this work has empowered my life, and I want to help people empower theirs. I have spoken to many people who are fascinated by reincarnation or their past lives but are hesitant to try regression. I want the people who are awakening, who are searching, to realize what their lives are really about and what their true purpose is. I want them to understand that events in their lives no longer have to hold them back, that relationships with people, both loving and distant, can be thoroughly explored and healed if necessary.

It is my hope that this book will alleviate that hesitation. It is not filled with clinical research or case studies. It is meant to be easy to read and to provide glimpses into what you might gain from regression therapy. I believe that by sharing my personal experiences, it will help you become familiar with me and create a comfort level so that you will be able to share your own personal experiences with me. I hope the experiences I share from some of my clients will teach you the types of things you can explore and learn through regression. If you decide to try regression therapy, I want you to have an amazing experience, completely unlike my first experience, described in chapter 1.

When I work with someone who has an amazing session, he or she experiences so much learning and healing on so many levels. Getting answers to questions from his or her Spirit guides is just so inspiring for that person and for me. Some people leave a session and say, "Well, that was interesting," while others say, "I think I knew that on some level, but what a great confirmation," and others say, "This has changed my life." That final statement leaves me in awe.

Often, I get an email the next day from people telling me just how profound their session was, and I am so happy for them. I feel connected to them, and I know we are all one. I would love to know where their spiritual journey has taken them after a week, a month or a year. And many do keep in touch.

Studying energy healing and regression was not the beginning of my spiritual journey, however. Ten years previously, one of my daughters suffered from a traumatic incident. She didn't tell anyone because she didn't want us to worry. So she kept it all inside until she had a breakdown.

It was one of the hardest times of my life, and hers as well. I was the mom; I thought I was supposed to fix it for her. But I couldn't. For two years I watched her struggle, fall and get up just to fall again. No matter what idea I came up with to help her, nothing worked. She rebelled against everything I tried to do to help. I didn't realize at the time that she had to be the one to help herself.

At the same time, my marriage of 24 years, already on shaky ground, fell apart. I was raising my three daughters alone and working a very demanding job in a large marketing agency. No stress in my life! It is said that people are religious because they are afraid to go to hell, but people are spiritual because they have already been there. I was in hell.

One of the benefits of my job was that they would reimburse us for a gym membership to help relieve stress. I asked if I could substitute a gym membership for meditation classes. They agreed. I am a firm believer that when the student is ready, the teacher will come. I found an amazing teacher and studied with her for five years. I learned about my chi, my chakras and how to meditate, which I truly believe saved my sanity. I learned how to remain calm. I had two other daughters at home that deserved my love and attention. I had to keep myself strong for all of us.

I'm sharing this, which I lovingly refer to as the black hole in my life, because it set me on a journey. Although I believe I was always a spiritual person, meditation set me on my spiritual journey. I became insatiable. I read every book I could find. I went to expos and took classes. One thing led to another. I studied yoga, reiki, energy healing, chakra clearing, crystal healing, intuition, NLP and communication with Spirit before I even started my regression practice. I have had amazing teachers and wonderful experiences that healed many issues in my current life as well as past lives. All of this learning comes into practice at certain times during my regression work.

I am happy to say that my daughter who had the breakdown healed with time and is now a very spiritual woman, often teaching me things that she has learned. My youngest daughter is no longer modelling but still works in the fashion and entertainment industry as a hair and makeup artist. My middle daughter lives near Ottawa with her husband and daughters. And thankfully, I am no longer in hell.

As you read through the sections of this book, you will get a better understanding of how regression and Spirit-contact therapy can help you. The next section will focus on past life regression. I will explain how regression works through hypnosis, what karma is really all about and how you can find healing through forgiveness.

Section three explains between-life regression and our soul's journey, where we are in between our incarnations on earth. It explains our lives as pure Spirit, where we plan our next life and how we progress as a soul. Section four delves into fascinating examples of lives beyond earth and messages channelled from Spirit. In any example of my clients' experiences, I do not identify them by name; if names are given for clarification, they have been changed.

There are many things that I cannot explain, and so you will not find them in this book. But I work from my heart and trust that more knowledge will come. Maybe it will not be in this lifetime, but beyond. I do know, however, that I have learned so much from where I was 20 or 30 years ago. And this is the knowledge I share in this book. I share many personal details about my own life and am probably opening myself up to some criticism in doing so. But I am writing this from a place of love, and because I feel compelled to do so. If I can help just one person, then it will be worth it.

Although you may not agree with some of the information in this book or find it hard to believe, it is written in the way I have learned from amazing teachers, from remarkable regressions and information imparted by Spirit guides. At no time do I offer this information as undeniable proof. We must as individuals take responsibility for our own truths. It is my hope, however, that you will read it with an open mind, that much of it will resonate with you and that you feel it in your heart.

Please note that regression is only one way to find purpose and healing; however, it is a way that is often overlooked. This work is not meant to replace the advice of a physician, psychotherapist or any health-care professional. But if you seek knowledge beyond the everyday, beyond your current life, then I encourage you to experience a past life or between-life regression with the opportunity to meet your Spirit guides. It is an experience you will never forget.

SECTION 2

Past Life Learnings

CHAPTER 3

Past Life Regression

Our body is just a vehicle for us while we're here.
It is our soul and our spirit that last forever.
—Brian L. Weiss

I LOVE THIS WORK THAT I do. Every regression is so different. I never know what to expect. I meditate regularly and before each regression ask for guidance and the presence of my Spirit guides to be with me. I rely heavily on this guidance I receive intuitively through my higher self.

I do it because I know how much going through that spontaneous past life helped me understand things in my life. It motivated me to understand more. However, I do not want people to experience a past life the way I experienced my spontaneous past life. I ensure their memories are retrieved without pain or extreme emotions of fear or sadness.

The more I studied the more fascinated I became. I also know that I learn something new with every regression. It has changed the way I view life and what I understand about life after life—that we are spirits having a human experience, not humans having an occasional spiritual experience.

I want everyone to understand this. We do not have just one chance to get our life right, despite the circumstances we are born into, or suffer eternal damnation as many Christian religions teach. I grew up Christian and took my daughters to church. But I could never understand why a loving God would only give us one chance to get life right and then have us incarnate into so many different circumstances. I believe we progress with every lifetime—eternal progression. We learn at a rate that we are comfortable with. We set our own course and have the free will to live it, or have the opportunity to try again in another lifetime. This is the best reason I know for multiple lives, for reincarnation.

I am not against religion. I believe most religions are well meaning and offer people faith, hope and community, and that most people who go to church are wonderful and sincere. However, I also believe that many religions have changed their teachings from their origin to messages that control the masses through fear rather than love. I also believe Jesus came to earth as an exalted being, who came to change the world through his teachings of love, forgiveness and healing. Many people have asked to regress to the time when Jesus walked the earth. Those sessions are beautiful, and I love being able to share that experience with them.

I am being honest here when I admit the more I know, the more I realize I don't know. I still have so many questions. I still hope to keep learning for the rest of my life and for eternity. I question things, such as when we experience past lives, do we see things as they actually were? For example, when clients connect to their angels, are the angels actually very tall, beautiful beings with large wings, or is that just how they imagine angels would be? During my regressions, I believe I have seen things in a way that I could understand them. In a past life when I was a monk, did I really look like the stereotypical monk?—a rather rotund man, slightly balding, wearing a brown robe held together with a rope belt. I believe this was more metaphorical. That is what my impression of what a monk looked like in the 13th century, so that I knew I was a monk. But there are other images that I have seen that I know are true images. Sometime we see ourselves in past lives as an observer where we see ourselves as a separate being, and sometimes we see them as if we are actually there and looking through our eyes. I believe it doesn't really matter how we perceive our memories; it is what we understand and learn from them that is important.

There are many philosophies that say all our lives are happening simultaneously. This is a hard concept to understand because our lives on earth are so linear from birth to death. Are all our lifetimes parallel? Is time only an earthly construct? Days and nights are created by the spin of the Earth; seasons and years exist because Earth rotates around the sun. But when we aren't on Earth, when we are in spirit, does the sun always shine, with no nights, seasons or years?

There is an analogy that makes it easier to understand with each lifetime represented by a car driving on a very long and winding road. One car cannot see the cars in front of it or the cars behind it, but they are there. If you look at that road from a higher perspective, as from the heavens, you can see several of the cars all travelling on the road at the same time. This analogy may make it easier to envision, but again, I don't have a complete understanding of this.

I do want to share the things I have learned and what I understand about past life regression. There have been so many unforgettable lifetimes experienced by people during this altered state. I am amazed and feel honoured and often humbled to have shared their past lives with them.

I have met so many amazing people with amazing stories. Stories of love and loss. People who have had real angels help them during specific trials in their lives. People who have overcome terrible tragedies. Those who want nothing more than to be of service, and those looking for guidance or confirmation they are on the right path.

A man who wanted to experience a past life regression did not know how to go about it. A friend of his told him he found my website, and he immediately called me. We spoke over the phone a fair bit before he came for a session. During these conversations he told me he was completely blind. During his regression, he was able to see everything very clearly in his mind's eye and had an amazing experience. We have become friends, and he is still such an inspiration to me.

One day, a woman contacted me about an appointment for herself and her twin sister. They were turning 50 and to celebrate this milestone, they wanted to give each other special presents not of a material nature. Her sister gave them both an ancestry DNA test, which of course identified them as twins. So she decided to give them both past life regressions. Their appointments were scheduled for the same day, but they would not talk to each other until both regressions were completed. I was truly amazed when the second sister went to the same past life as her sister, who had come earlier. They were brothers in that life and had some similar characteristics that they have today. It was obvious to me that it was the same lifetime, as they were both in a flour mill that one of the brothers owned. Afterwards they told me even more details of that life, and of another same lifetimes they both experienced that I hadn't even recognized.

People rarely find that they were anyone famous in a past life, or even linked to a famous person. Most discover everyday lives. But they do find themselves in fascinating times. Lives in ancient

Egypt or ancient Greece are always interesting. Many people living in this area have experienced lives as North American natives. I love when I receive emails afterwards with pictures attached that they researched on the Internet of the exact type of house they lived in, types of art that they created or uniforms they wore. These types of confirmations make the experience more real for them.

The following is an example of a past life regression. Some extremely personal information has been left out and names have been changed. I chose to share this regression for many reasons. It shows a pattern in Jane's current life that stemmed from previous lifetimes, and how connecting to her Spirit guide afterwards helped give her a better understanding of how they influenced her current life. Notice how at times Jane told me what she was observing in her past life. Sometimes she spoke in first person, and when connecting to Spirit, her voice changed slightly and her Spirit guide spoke through her.

Jane is in her mid-50s. Her main concerns were an issue with weight and her relationship with her husband, Paul. After hypnotizing her, I asked to speak directly to her subconscious mind to see if there were emotional issues in this life that caused her to overeat. It became apparent it had a lot to do with her relationship with her husband.

I asked her subconscious to take her to the past lives that were the cause of the problems she had with Paul. Her memories came fast and easy. In the first life, she found herself, as a black female in Africa, sitting in the doorway of a mud hut. She could see a sick child on the floor and a pot of stale water in the corner. Her husband was the same soul as Paul. He was standing around talking with the other men of the village. He would not go to the well for water, and this made Jane angry. The well had dried up, and the men of the town just stood around talking and laughing, but would not dig another well. She had walked two kilometres to another well just two days ago.

Going forward to the next major event in that life, she was walking with two women from the town where they lived, her dead baby in her arms. They were going to bury the child. The men continued to do nothing but stand around and talk. She was furious.

"I will not have sex with that man again. There will be no more children," she said quite adamantly.

After experiencing that life, she went to another lifetime that she also shared with Paul. She saw herself behind the bar of an inn at the end of the 18th century. She was the innkeeper. Her husband (same soul as Paul) worked on a ship. Every time his ship came in, he would come to the inn. But he didn't help; he talked and partied with the other men. Their relationship was very sexual. Jane loved him but felt much anger and resentment towards him during this lifetime as well.

We explored a third lifetime that she shared with this same soul, as well as the souls of her daughter and sister in her current life. She was a little girl living on a farm in one of the prairie provinces of Canada. She felt the wind coming in through the windows. She had a little brother whom she loved very much. Her mother was harsh. I asked why her why, and Jane explained that her mother was very disappointed because her husband was so mean. He would not give her any love, and the children were unwanted.

During this lifetime in the prairies, Jane's mother was the same soul as her daughter in her current life. Her little brother, Georgie,

18

was her present-day sister, and her father was the same soul as Paul.

Jane stopped speaking to me and spoke to her little brother. She was actually speaking as the little girl and not as Jane. "Don't worry, Georgie, I will take care of you."

I asked her what was happening.

"My mother is leaving us. My father left us too. We are only 11 and 7 years old, and we are afraid. We are taken to the orphanage. Mrs Harkness, the schoolmarm, needs a young boy to work on her farm. She adopted Georgie. But I was never adopted. I was older and able to help Mrs Becker with the children at the orphanage. When Mrs Becker died of consumption, I took over the orphanage. I never married but found peace in caring for the children. I never saw my parents again."

It was obvious Jane and Paul had created a pattern throughout these lifetimes, which continued into their current life. By connecting to her higher self and calling in her Spirit guide, Jane gained an understanding of the lifetimes she had just experienced. I realized Jane was channelling when she began speaking about herself in the third person.

Her guide, Ashram, informed me that she is Jane's deceased mother from her current life. They had made a pact before she died that she would stay close to Jane. She is wise and seemingly without gender. Ashram is speaking through Jane.

> I am a member of Jane's soul family. I am with her constantly. Jane has gained this weight to help her understand. If she had stayed the

way she was in her past life, she would not learn to help others empathically. She was very beautiful, but she used that beauty to be manipulative. When issues unfolded before her, she dealt with them in a manipulative manner. This beauty was taken away, so that she would learn how to deal from a place of empathy. But now there are many concerns; it has gone beyond what it should have and is affecting her health.

Jane's health will be given back. She must be there for others to serve and give. She has learned to love a great deal. She has almost loved too much, which has disabled her family. They have become dependent. She needs to learn to let go; this stems from her ego issues.

Paul is walking the path of the unreliable husband. His lesson is to learn to love from his heart. He has made progress in this life, but he has a rim of cold, like ice, around his heart. This is from an experience five lifetimes ago. Jane has chosen to have the gift of empathy. But her love is too unconditional. It must be more conditional; she is enabling his demands.

Jane is a transitioner. She is going to help other souls in passing from this life to the next. She has much to do and many miles to go. Jane should understand that she is loved and watched over. She should continue her readings and develop her channelling to come forth with love and understanding. So it is. Our Blessings.

Ashram spoke fast, much faster than Jane. She did not leave much time to question things, and when she was done, that was it, she was gone. I sensed that she was loving but also really direct.

Once I brought Jane back into the room, she understood what her deceased mother/guide was telling her, and not just from the message above but from all that she felt and understood while receiving the message. More than I could understand from just hearing the words. This is how Spirit communication works.

Not everyone who regresses will channel. Although it is no surprise when someone does channel, most people don't. Typically, time spent with Spirit guides is more of a question- and-answer session that also includes healing, encouragement, counselling and much love. All regressions, as different as they are, are interesting, informative, healing and offer messages from Spirit guides.

CHAPTER 4

My Process

WHEN AN APPOINTMENT IS MADE for a regression, I start days ahead of time. During my daily meditation, I ask that this person has the best experience possible for his or her highest good. I keep the energy in my room high and set up a healing circle before the person arrives to keep the atmosphere optimal for every session. I ask my guides to be with me at all times, because this work is very intuitive.

I regress through hypnosis, and people often wonder if they can be hypnotized. Some wonder if they were actually hypnotized, because they had preconceived ideas about what hypnosis is. I always have a pre-regression talk with clients to explain how hypnosis works, the whole process and, of course, to understand what they want to get out of a session. This talk usually lasts about an hour but can be shorter or longer depending on how chatty the client is. I do not put a time limit on a regression so there is no pressure to worry about how long it takes, which is usually about three hours. If a client is having an amazing conversation with their Spirit guides, I am certainly not going to be the one to say, "Sorry, time's up"!

There are a few people who have not had a successful regression, but this is quite rare. A few people have come with deep-seated religious backgrounds and felt guilty about what they were doing, which prevented their success. Some were type A or very skeptical personalities that could not grasp the idea of letting go and just letting it happen. But most people who come are already spiritually minded, meditate or have already tried other modalities, such as energy healing. Most people have amazing sessions.

Hypnosis enables the mind to travel across the dimension of time. This is how it works for regression. There are two stages of hypnosis: induction and suggestion. During induction, brainwaves slow from beta to alpha and then theta. Beta is our normal, waking state when we are actively engaged; our brainwaves range from 15 to 40 cycles per second. During alpha, the brainwaves slow from 9 to 14 cycles per second; this happens when we relax, daydream, meditate or just chill out. A theta state slows the brainwaves to 5 to 8 cycles per second; it occurs between wakefulness and sleep, a state where answers to problems just seem to appear. When we are in delta, a deep, dreamless sleep, brainwaves slow to 2 to 4 cycles per second. Studies have proven that there are differences in brain activity during hypnosis. Some areas of the brain become less active, while connections in other areas of the brain become stronger.

I like to take clients deep into hypnosis so they have an excellent experience. Somewhere between alpha and theta is the hypnogogic state, optimal for regression. A trance-like state, when a heightened state of focus is obtained. During this state, people are more open to suggestion and can access their subconscious minds, where the memories of all of their past lives are stored. The relaxed state enables one to access and review memories that they normally aren't aware of or have forgotten or repressed. Being open to suggestion allows me to direct them to their desired past lives.

There are so many different types of lifetimes that can be explored. Many people know what they want to explore, while others just aren't sure. Lifetimes can be explored to see if there is a connection between you and another person—a family member, a love interest, someone you have an immediate or very strong connection to or someone you just can't seem to get along with. Unexplained fears, such as claustrophobia, or health conditions, such as migraines, could be caused by past life trauma. Extreme interest in certain time periods, such as ancient civilizations, different cultures or other countries could stem from past lives. Some people like to explore what type of person they were in other lives, such as if they were a leader, a healer or had a particular talent. Often, I suggest they explore the lifetime that is the most significant to their current life.

After the pre-talk, I begin by guiding clients through a deep relaxation, followed by a chakra visualization. This helps them to start visualizing, and energizes and balances the chakras that will help them through the experience. Next is the hypnotic induction, followed by the journey through a tunnel to a significant scene in a past life. When they step out of the tunnel, they will remember the first past life they have asked to explore. Much is included during this induction to surround clients with divine white light and protection during their session.

People perceive their memories in different ways. Many see their past lives like a movie; this is clairvoyance. Others do not see a movie but get several visuals or pictures. With the visuals comes an understanding, a download of memories or a clear knowing, and this is claircognizance.

Most people will feel things. For example, if they suffered a heart attack in a past life, they may feel pressure in their chest area. They do not experience pain. This is clairsentience or clear feelings. Also, with clairsentience, they feel emotions. The emotions often appear on their face before they even mention what is happening.

I like to tell them afterwards that this is how they know they were not making it up. They would not feel the emotions if the memory did not resonate with them on some level.

They may also experience clairaudience, which is hearing sounds, talking or music. Taste and smell can also be triggered while remembering. There is usually a combination of all these perceptions, so it is important to pay attention to everything they are experiencing, even if it may seem strange at the time. The best advice I can give them is to stay out of their left brain, where ego resides. The ego is critical, analytical, fearful and sceptical. It can make them believe they are making things up. The more they trust what they are perceiving, the easier and faster the memories come.

Since they are now open to suggestion, it is important to not lead or suggest to them as to what they are perceiving. This is done by only asking open-ended questions. I let them tell me what they remember. Once they are trusting, it is easy to take them forward or backward in that life. I can bring them back to their current life and then on to another past life. Usually, we explore three past lives during a session, which we have determined during the pre-talk.

During a regression, even though people are connected to their subconscious minds, their conscious mind is always aware of what is happening and of their present life. So I can ask if they recognize anyone from their current life, who could be a spouse or a child, but in their past life they could be someone completely different and even a different sex. A husband could be a wife, a child could be a friend or grandparent and so on. They are not recognizing the person; they are recognizing the soul. If they are clearly seeing other people, they can look into the eyes, which are the window to the soul. Even if they do not see the person clearly, they can still recognize the soul. It always amazes me how this works.

After experiencing the third past life, I guide clients to their superconscious mind, their higher-self, and they call in their Spirit guides. When our souls come to earth and take on a body, there is always a portion of our soul that remains in Spirit world. This is our higher self. It is by connecting to our higher self that we receive intuition and connect to Spirit guides, angels, teachers and other beings of light.

There are so many ways people become aware of their guides. Some see them in human form, or kind of filmy, like a ghost. Many see them as angels or deceased loved ones. They often appear as Native Americans, animals, orbs, energy and have even appeared as extraterrestrial. Others don't see them at all but feel their presence and connect telepathically. What is most common, though, is the unconditional love they feel. If more than one guide appears, we ask one to step forward to be a spokesperson (or spoke-Spirit) for the group. We always ask for a name of the guide that we can address them with. This also allows the person to call upon them by name afterwards. The conversation between client and guide is telepathic, but the client repeats it back to me so that I can understand the message and so they have it on their recording. We discuss what kind of questions they want to ask during the pre-talk. It often happens that they are overwhelmed when they feel the unconditional love, they are happy to just be in their guide's presence. I help them to remember what they wanted to ask.

During this meeting they get an explanation of how the past lives they just remembered affect their current life. It is also the time when forgiveness and erasing karma occurs. Questions are answered often having to do with life's purpose, next steps, relationships or why they are experiencing certain issues. I have them ask their guide(s) for a healing when necessary. These healings happen in a variety of ways, including the laying on of hands and administering light and warmth. They are always beautiful experiences. Being connected to Spirit guides is also the time when most channelling will occur.

I believe the client gets so much more understanding from meeting their Spirit guides than if they just remembered their past lives. I am always honoured and often humbled to be part of this most intimate and beautiful Spirit guide experience.

CHAPTER 5

Karma

> How people treat you is their karma; how you
> react is yours.
>
> —Wayne Dyer

IT IS NOT MY INTENT here to prove that reincarnation exists. There is enough evidence and case studies on the Internet that will convince you if you are not sure. If reincarnation did not exist, there would be no reason to do a past life regression; in fact, it would not be possible.

What Is Karma?

Karma is the reason for reincarnation and helps us understand how we are all connected—part of everything and everyone around us. Most people misunderstand karma and believe it is punishment for something they have done wrong. It is not punishment, and understanding what karma really is can be a powerful tool for self-development. I do not want to go into a deep Buddhist philosophy here, but rather to explain how karma ties into regression therapy. Karma is the way we grow and evolve spiritually. It is meant to be resolved, not relived. It has no timeline.

Karma is a Sanskrit word meaning action. It refers to the law of cause and effect. If you plant an apple tree, you will not get oranges from it, only apples. If you plant an acorn, an oak tree will grow. The tree then produces more acorns and the cycle continues. If you do not plant the acorn, no oak tree can grow. Therefore, the law of karma dictates that if you act positively, you will experience harmony. If you act negatively, you will experience disharmony. The vibrations you send out to the universe will always come back to you.

You create your own karma or reality as a response to everything you think, say or do. All your talents, abilities, problems and afflictions are a result of your programming, not only in this life but in all your past lives. In understanding this, you accept self-responsibility. If you are responsible for everything that has happened to you, then you realize you also are responsible for the opportunities to overcome them.

This is a hard concept for many to understand, but stay with me. If you are responsible for everything that happens in your life, there is no one else to blame. Karma contradicts blame. You cannot be a victim. Think about all the problems you have suffered through and how they have made you stronger and more compassionate. Have you ever met someone who has led a pampered life? He or she can seem self-absorbed or superficial.

If you want to know how you are doing with karma during your current life, you only have to ask yourself if you are living a life of positivity and unconditional love, or one of blame and negativity. How do you react when things go wrong? Do you hold on to anger, judge people or get motivated by revenge, greed or power? Don't be too hard on yourself if these emotions happen. These questions are just meant to get you thinking. If you have not completely reached the "unconditional love for all of mankind" stage, you have all the lifetimes you need to achieve it. This is the most important message I try to give to my clients. You don't have to do it all in your current life or suffer eternal damnation in a hell filled with fire and brimstone. These are manmade, medieval concepts developed to control the masses, and unfortunately, they are still very effective for many people today.

Does this mean we must justify crime, poverty, inequality, violence? No, and this is how I came to understand reincarnation and karma. Brought up Catholic, we were sent to church, not taken to church. My father had a grocery store and worked on Sundays, so he was obviously going to hell in a handbag! My mother converted to Catholicism to marry my father, so her heart was not in it. My brother and sister would take the coins from their weekly offering envelopes, go sit at the snack bar at the local drug store and drink Coke until church and Sunday school were over. But I would go to church, which was mostly in Latin back then, and then to Sunday school to be taught by the nuns.

I believed everything they told me. My purpose in life was to serve God, but if I dared miss church on Sunday, I was going to hell. At least I would be with the rest of my family, right? As I grew older and started to think about what I had been taught, I had a lot of questions. If we only had one life to live, why were some people born rich and others poor? Why were children starving in Africa? Why were people born with severe handicaps? Why were children who were born and not baptized not allowed to enter heaven? Why was my grandfather, who was divorced and remarried, and the rest of my family going to hell? Why did people die young, get disease, or, even worse, get raped or murdered? Why would a loving God only give us one chance to get it right or have us suffer eternal damnation?

Why? Why? Why?

As I understand now, we don't only have one life to live, one life to grow spiritually. We all have an innate desire to improve ourselves and raise our vibration with each incarnation. Reincarnation gives us as many lifetimes as it takes for us to attain enough spiritual growth so that we no longer have to incarnate on earth. It gives us the opportunity to review each life and decide what we need to work on in the next incarnation. So that is my belief of what karma is all about—understanding and spiritual growth.

If we all have this innate desire to improve ourselves, I couldn't understand why there were still bad people on earth. This became clear to me with a simplistic analogy of earth lives being like a school explained to me by my Spirit guides. Some people are in grade one, some in grade six, some in high school, some in university and all the grades in between. Younger souls could be likened to being in grade one, the older souls to the higher grades. You cannot expect a child in grade one to know as much as a child in grade six. A child just starting high school cannot possibly know as much or accept as much responsibility as a young adult in university. Being in grade one, or a younger soul, is neither right nor wrong, bad or good when compared to a high school student. A younger soul just has less experience with life lessons. And so, we are all at different stages of learning. We should never judge another's progress, or compare our own progress with someone we think is more advanced spiritually. There is more explanation of this in chapter 9 regarding soul evolution.

At some point after your soul ascends to Spirit world, you have a chance to review all your past lives in your Akashic records found in your book of life in the Great Hall or Library. When looking over these records, you might realize that you need more understanding in a certain area of your life, or you need to change some of the core beliefs you acquired over the last few lifetimes. When you create the plans for your next incarnation, you then create opportunities for your next life that will help you gain the understanding or change your core beliefs. The important thing to note is that you decide what you want to work on, how you want to work on it and when you are ready to work on it. These concepts are explained in more detail in the Between-Life Learnings in section 3.

There are flipsides to karma. It's not just about struggles. If you give love, compassion, gratitude and positivity, you will receive that in return. It can also help mitigate any existing karma you may have.

You may look at people who seems to have it all: talent, wealth, success and popularity. You may think they have no karma, but this may actually be a way they have decided to test themselves. How will they handle success? Will their ego take over? Will they be generous with their money? Will they be compassionate toward others?

Working with people during regression, we often explore why they have particular problems in their current lives by going back to the lifetime that caused the issue. This is, of course, if the issue was created in a past life. Sometimes they are not, so then while still in a hypnotic state, I may look for blocks in their chakras or try NLP (neurolinguistic programming) techniques to help them resolve the problem. But if the problem is related to an unresolved past life issue or karma, just uncovering the cause can start a healing process by helping alleviate the effect.

Different types of karma relate to regression therapy. They can help us understand how these issues can affect us.

Balancing Karma

This is mainly understood as cause and effect. How do we learn how to be a good person if we do not understand that harmful action is wrong? Understanding balancing karma can help us understand why bad things happen to good people. If there was no balancing karma, then there would be no consequences when we die. As evolving souls, we have all had past lives where we were not very nice.

One day during my training, we were regressed to a lifetime where we were the worst perpetrator of all our lifetimes. That was an eye opener. I saw myself working in the bottom of the Roman coliseum. I was nasty. I tormented the prisoners, and I loved to see them torn apart by animals or kill each other. I can honestly say that I know I have evolved from that lifetime. I can't even look at roadkill now. Interesting side note: after that we regressed to the worst lifetime we experienced as a victim (I know I said earlier that there really are no victims, but this is how the teacher regressed us). Two people in my class of just 12 found themselves in the coliseum in their lifetimes as the biggest victim. I apologized profusely to them, in case we were there at the same time.

An example of balancing karma would be people who were racist or anti-gay in their past life. They may have caused someone or many people to suffer because of their opinions or actions. After a life review, they would realize the effect this attitude had on others and the suffering it caused. To understand what they had done on a deep soul level, so that they will never express or even have this attitude again, they may choose to come back as a person in a minority group or someone from the LGBTQ community. The expected outcome of choosing this next life from the side of the oppressed would hopefully result in a life of compassion or altruistic work. Of course, when we incarnate we go through a forgetting, so there is a possibility that they could take on a victim attitude or be angry and not learn the planned lessons. If this was the case, they could decide another way to try balancing the karma again in the next life, or try working it out over a few lifetimes in ways where they would have more success.

Another example would be a man who deliberately disabled someone. He could decide to come back disabled to balance his karma. Balancing karma is required if the offence was done deliberately, not accidentally.

Jane, who you read about earlier, was told by her guide that she was very beautiful in past lives but used that beauty to manipulate men. She decided to come back in this life without the beauty so she would not be tempted to manipulate men again.

Balancing karma may also require some absolution from the souls of the individuals who were disabled or oppressed. It is important to note that not all people who are of a minority group, gay, disabled or part of any marginalized group are that way because they are balancing karma.

Balancing karma can also be a beautiful way to return an act of kindness to someone. In a past life, my husband was my father who changed his life completely to help me at a time when I needed healing. In this current lifetime, I wanted to be here as a support for him through some of his challenges.

Physical Karma

When someone dies a traumatic or accidental death, it can leave an energetic imprint on his or her soul. A woman who was crushed to death when a building collapsed may be claustrophobic in her current life. A child who died of smoke inhalation during a

35

fire may come back with asthma. I have heard of a case where doctors could find no reason for a woman experiencing migraine headaches, and recommended she stay on medication for the rest of her life. During a regression she found she was hit over the head with a rock until she died. Just discovering the cause eliminated the effect, and her migraines disappeared.

Dr Ian Stevenson, a psychiatrist at the University of Virginia and pioneer of reincarnation research, studied children from all over the world who remembered past lives. In a study, he noted that 35 per cent of children who remembered a past life identified a birthmark corresponding to a fatal wound they had received in their past life. His 1997 book, *Reincarnation and Biology Volume 1: Birthmarks,* cites many fascinating instances of these children.

I have a birthmark on my lower back that is the shape of a map of Australia. During my studies, one of my classmates regressed me to see if it was from a past life incident. I went back to an encounter with a bear that gave me a fatal slash across that part of my back with his very large paw.

False-Fear Karma

I see this often. When someone has an unexplainable and extreme fear, it could be caused by a traumatic past life event. It can often be expressed in reoccurring dreams or nightmares. During REM sleep, our brainwaves slow down to the theta level, and we connect to our subconscious mind, where the memory of all of our past lives resides. Dreams that cause you to panic or give you anxiety, especially if they are reoccurring dreams, are often past life related. I worked with a woman who constantly had terrifying dreams of being in a house fire and was not able to get out. We were able to sort that out by going back to the past life where this had actually happened.

Another example of a false fear happened when I regressed a friend of mine. She has three sons, and her husband bought a 40-foot sailboat so they could spend summers sailing on Lake Ontario. On the first trip out, she hated it. She could not stand the sound of the sails flapping in the wind or the feeling of being so vulnerable out on the water far away from the shore. We decided to see if this was caused by a past life event. I directed her back to the lifetime that was the cause of this fear. She found herself on a dock, which seemed to be in England during the 1800s, although she felt that she was Dutch because she was wearing wooden shoes. She and her husband were boarding a tall ship to sail to the Americas to start a new life.

I took her forward to the next major event. People were panicking and rushing down the steps, while she was running up to the deck to find her husband. There was a terrible storm at sea. The sails had ripped and were flailing uncontrollably, causing the ship to pitch back and forth. Suddenly the mast broke, which cause the ship to capsize. Everyone drowned. Once she understood where the fear originated, and that the fear was not caused by anything in her current life, it did not have the same power over her. Since I regress through hypnosis, I was then able to give her hypnotic suggestions that her family would not be going out on the lake in bad weather and they would all be safe. It took a few sails for her to be completely comfortable, but she was able to spend the summer on the boat with her family.

Two completely different women on different occasions came to me with a weight issue. During their past life exploration, they both went back to lives where they were prostitutes. They did not work in a house where they were kept but were on their own in the streets. They had very little money, only enough for food and shelter, and food was scarce. When they were able to buy or find it, they gorged themselves because they never knew when they would get their next meal. One of the women had even brought food to her session, in case it went too long. This was the understanding as to why they overate consistently. Releasing the cause helped eliminate the effect. I suggested that each of them join a weight-loss program as soon as possible. I do not always hear back from clients, so I hope they had success. But I do know that one of the women had lost enough weight in the following two weeks to wear a dress to a Christmas party that she had previously outgrown.

False-Guilt Karma

False-guilt karma can occur when people feel responsible for a tragic event in a past life when they really were not to blame. An example of this is a man who was a workaholic. His family wanted him to spend less time at the office and more time with them. However, he felt he needed to put in as many hours as possible so that he could provide for them. In a regression he found out that there was a drought during one of his lifetimes. His crops failed and his family starved to death. Although this was no fault of his own, he subconsciously felt that if he didn't work harder in his current life, his family would suffer again.

False-guilt karma is rather personal to me. I have always had a guilty conscious, even at times when I wasn't guilty. During a between-life regression, I found myself sitting outside as a monk in about the thirteenth century. I looked very much like the stereotypical monk, in a brown robe with a rope tied around my waist. I was quite rotund and balding on the top of my head. As I mentioned previously, I am not sure if this is what I actually looked like. I believe our subconscious sometimes gives us these glimpses in a way that we will understand them, rather than as they actually were.

I lived in the king's court and was very much respected and loved by the royal family. I provided food to the court that required fermenting, like cheese and wine (two of my favourite things today). One day the princess ate or drank something I had prepared and died. Had I not been so loved by the royal family; I would have been beheaded immediately. But instead, they threw me in the dungeon where I was left and forgotten about until the day I died. I can still see myself sitting on the floor, my one hand manacled to the wall. Needless to say, I went mad with grief and guilt.

This took place during a between-life regression, and I was taken to the day of my death during that lifetime. (Read about between-life regressions in section 3.) I did not cross over into the Spirit world immediately. Instead, I remained earthbound, hovering over the kitchens where I stayed until I felt comfortable enough that the next person fermenting the same foods I had made was doing it correctly so no one else would die.

The first place I went when I finally did cross over was into a beautiful garden to receive healing. Then my guide took me to the Great Library or Akashic records, where I was able to review my book of life. I looked through my past lives and saw that I had been carrying this guilt around with me for centuries.

I then asked my guide if I could meet my soul group. He seemed stern and would not take me anywhere until I agreed to lock that guilt up into the book and stop carrying it around with me from lifetime to lifetime. I did this but felt such a conflict. I literally had trouble leaving that book and the guilt behind. It was a real struggle. It seemed to me that I was actually addicted to that karmic guilt.

When I finally was able to let the book go, the whole countenance on my guide's face changed. He took me to meet my soul group, and they all cheered and said how happy they were that I was finally able to let that go. They told me I needed to do that before I could successfully realize my purpose, which is the regression work that I now do. What a confirmation! That also explains why I love this work so much.

The Karma of Talent

Many times, people ask me if they had certain talents, leadership qualities or healing skills in a past life. It's wonderful to know that it's not just the issues that we bring with us from one life to the next but also the talents and learnings. It's not surprising that so many women who are energy workers or practice alternative modalities have found themselves to be healers in past lives.

There are so many children that we see today who are prodigies, and bringing the talent with them is the best explanation. Some examples are children younger than age 10 going to university or creating beautiful works of art. Wayne Gretzky and Tiger Woods showed incredible athletic ability while they were still very young. Mozart could play the piano and violin at 3 years old and composed his first piano concerto at the age of 4.

One day I received an email asking if I could hypnotize people who were 86 years old. I replied that I had hypnotized my mother when she was 88, and I was willing to give it a try. I offered this woman a few books to read before her session so she would have some understanding of what it would be like.

When I took them to her house, she invited me in. She had beautiful art all over her walls, and I don't just mean some nice paintings. I mean incredible works of art created in many different mediums. I later found out that the art was all original pieces that she had painted herself. She wanted to see if she had painted in a past life. She knew that her grandfather had been an artist in Great Britain, but he had died before she was born so she never had a chance to meet him. When he moved to Canada, he taught art at the university level. One of his students was actually a member of the Group of Seven, a group of very famous Canadian artists.

When she explored her past lives, she discovered that she was actually the same soul as her grandfather, who she found to be a rather gruff fellow. She had brought that art talent with her into this lifetime. We became good friends, had incredible conversations and even shared books until, sadly, she crossed over this year. I am lucky to have two of her pieces of art today.

We transcend karma in this life or past lives by understanding what we did and taking responsibility for it. We must then set the intention to break the cycle, making conscious decisions not to act or react in the same way again in the next incarnation. We must also forgive and make amends if necessary and find opportunities to create positive actions that will help and inspire others. Karma being the law of cause and effect, however, also dictates that if you live a life of love, kindness and service, that is what you will receive in return.

It is my understanding that once we humans have ascended into the 5th dimensional consciousness and the new earth, the law of karma will be transmuted and we will no longer carry karmic debt.

CHAPTER 6

Forgiveness

To err is human, to forgive, divine.
                              —Alexander Pope, 1711

When one forgives, two souls are set free.
                              —Unknown

ONE OF THE MOST IMPORTANT tools for healing during regression, and in life, is forgiveness. Forgiveness detaches us from the suffering of the past. It allows us to release anger, hurt and bitterness. It frees our soul and releases karma. Forgiveness does not mean we condone something someone did to us, but forgiving absolves the power another person has over us. It makes us stronger and teaches us to create boundaries, so we will not be harmed again.

I learned the wisdom of forgiveness after I went through a divorce. My husband of 24 years and I separated. I was now a single mother with three children and a low-paying job. I am not saying I was completely innocent in this marriage. I am a pretty strong-willed person. But I felt overwhelmed. After a while, I realized my marriage was over and I could either become a victim, or I could move on. What happened, happened. I could not change it, and not forgiving him would not change it. Yet, there were days when I was hurt and frustrated as a single mother, while he went off to be happy with someone new and younger.

Then one day, I am not sure exactly how or when it happened, but I became aware that by forgiving him I released any power he had over me. It freed me, and I realized I was happier alone than living with someone who no longer loved me. Looking back, I can now see with clarity that I was better off, and after exploring our relationship during a regression, I found out why my marriage failed. I explain this in the chapter 8 regarding spiritual contracts.

Working with regression assists people with forgiveness when necessary and starts the healing process. A woman who came to me had some issues enjoying sex. She did not mind having sex with her partner but didn't really find any pleasure in it. In one of the lifetimes she experienced, she found herself being abducted by a group of villains in the time of the American old west. They used her for their own enjoyment until she found a way to escape. I thought this may have been the reason for her lack of enjoyment and had her forgive these men, which she had no problem doing. But as we went on, it came out she felt shame for enjoying sex with some of the men. This shame carried over to her current life. For this I worked with her to forgive herself. Forgiving others may be hard, but forgiving ourselves is often harder, and she found it more difficult to forgive herself. I explained that sexual gratification is a human nature, and even though those were not the best of circumstances, since she was with these men for a period of time, she would probably feel some pleasure, and she should not feel ashamed about it. Forgiveness of self is a powerful thing; it un-compromises our souls and alleviates guilt and shame.

There is a difference between guilt and shame. Guilt is feeling bad about something we have done. Shame is feeling bad about ourselves, which affects our self-esteem and makes us feel unworthy. It can cause abuse of self or others, rage or addiction.

Learning self-compassion, which is a part of self-forgiveness, allows us to let go of shame and start the healing process.

During another session, a woman regressed back to a life as an ancient Roman soldier. She found herself in the typical dress of sandals, short red skirt and helmet. She was a member of the army that was sent to arrest Jesus. Unsure of who he was, she felt he was just another criminal and carried out the orders to help crucify him. Later, as Jesus was hanging on the cross, she realized who he was and what he meant to his followers. She kept repeating, "I didn't know who he was; they lied to me; I didn't know." Her guilt was so strong in that life that after Jesus died she was filled with self-condemnation. She lived a lonely life, unable and unwilling to find love, and eventually died alone.

After she connected to her Spirit guide, he brought in another guide. It was Mary, the mother of Jesus. Mary took her to a pool of water where she went for healing. Mary sat on the edge of the pool and told her, "I have forgiven you, and my son has forgiven you. It is time to forgive yourself." She left her guilt in the healing water of the pool. Afterwards, she was sitting on the edge of the pool chatting with Mary. I am not always aware of all that goes on during these conversations, only what people report back to me. There are often long, quiet pauses during a regression. It was obvious that more healing was happening, so I did not interrupt with questions. When she started to speak again, she told me all was forgiven.

Forgiveness is usually asked for or given while people are connected to their Spirit guides, while ego seems to be unengaged in the background. Forgiveness of self is important so that we do not stay stuck in the past. Agonizing over things done in our recent past or a past life can not only cause anxiety and depression but affect our physical and mental health. Self-forgiveness helps us learn from our mistakes and frees us to move forward with our lives. Without the weight of self-loathing we have possibly been carrying around for lifetimes, we can literally transform our lives.

Understanding forgiveness helps us understand that nothing is done to us, but whatever happened has taught us a soul lesson and made us stronger.

SECTION 3

Between-Life Learnings

CHAPTER 7

Between-Life Soul Regression

> When the time comes, the journey toward the brilliant white light that marks the barrier between this world and the next will not hold as much fear as it once would have. For in my study of death, I have found the celebration of life.
>
> —Dolores Cannon

I HAD BEEN WORKING WITH past life regression for about two years when I went to a meditation to celebrate the vernal equinox. We shared ideas and talked about the different modalities we worked with. Someone asked me if I had ever heard of Dr Michael Newton and the work he did with life between lives. I hadn't. But as the Universe would have it, there just happened to be one copy of his book *Journey of Souls* for sale. I took it home and stayed up all night reading it. I can honestly say, this book has had more impact on me and my beliefs than any other book I have read to date. I had to know more! I studied with Dr Linda Backman of the Ravenheart Center in Boulder, Colorado. Linda had worked with Dr Newton, who was by then retired.

This fascinating work can answer so many more questions. What is my purpose? Am I on the right track? Have I completed my spiritual contracts? Why was I born into the family I have? It provides an understanding of our eternal life as a soul, of things that occurred in our life and of the choices we made before we were born. Things that happened to us or things we considered as failings can be seen from a soul level, and we can find that we had actually planned them as learning experiences.

The Process

Between-life regression requires taking the person being regressed to a much deeper level of hypnotic trance than is required for past life regression. I always make sure the person has experienced past life regression before exploring the between life. This way he or she has more understanding of how regression works. It does get easier the more you experience it.

The session starts by exploring the past life that is most significant to their current life. After getting an understanding of that past life, I take them to the last day of that lifetime. This is done without pain and extreme emotion. Then I bring them to the point right after death when their Spirit leaves their body and returns home to the Spirit world, as they have done so many times before. They are met by their Spirit guides, angels, soul group or deceased love ones. The Spirit realm is one of love and compassion. It is non-judgmental. Unconditional love is felt immediately. The Spirit guides usually take over at this time. They know what is best for the highest good of a person on a soul level.

Once someone has entered the Spirit realm, he or she experiences it as a pure soul, without human ego. Our ego is left behind with our body when we die. I facilitated a between-life regression for a dear friend whose brother had been murdered while working in the Caribbean. The only suspect was released and immediately left the islands. After being with her guides for a while, they took her to meet her brother. It was an incredibly joyful reunion. She was so happy to see him completely well. They embraced and then lay down in the grass holding hands, staring up at the sky. There was no need to discuss the murder or who the murderer was. All that mattered was that he was fine. Had she been coming from a place of ego, the identity of the murderer would have been her first question.

If someone has died from a traumatic experience or had a hard life, this person will often go to a place of healing first. This will often be in a garden or through a shower of luminous light. This helps to release any negative energy or exhaustion from the previous life before he or she is ready to move on. It's so very calming that people usually want to stay there for a while. People who have had extremely traumatic experiences may not want to incarnate back on earth for a while, or they may choose a different plane, perhaps a mental plane where they do not have to have a body. This is determined with the help of their Spirit guides or the Council of Elders.

The Akashic Records

Although there is no set order in what occurs while people are experiencing the Spirit realm, the next step is often a past life review, which usually happens by accessing the Akashic records that are kept in the Great Library or hall of records. The Akashic records are a multidimensional archive of every soul's journey that has existed since the beginning of life. Our own record is sometimes referred to as our book of life. The wisdom contained in these records contains all our thoughts, words and actions throughout all our lifetimes, as well as future possibilities. They connect us to each other. They help us understand what we have accomplished and what we still have to work on in our next incarnation for our soul's growth. These insights are recorded from a spiritual perspective without judgement, only love.

I saw the hall of records as a beautiful marble-columned building. It looked like an ancient Roman or Greek temple. Inside were rooms filled with rows and rows of books. A guide brought me my soul's book and set it on a table. There were no words on the pages, but when I opened it, I just knew or assimilated everything I needed to know from them. My experience there was unforgettable. I have explained it previously in the false-guilt karma section. I remember the encouragement I received from my soul group. They had actually told me that doing this regression work was a large part of my life purpose.

Much of what also can happen is explained in the next two chapters about meeting your soul group and pre-life planning.

Callings

In between-life regressions, we learn so many things about our current life and life in Spirit before we choose to incarnate again. We exist in both worlds at the same time. Our higher self, that part of our soul that remains in the Spirit world, continues to learn and progress on a spiritual level at the same time we do as humans on earth. As spirit, we actually attend lessons in classrooms with our soul group, and we have specific callings. Some help souls heal when they cross through the veil, others may work in the nursery with new souls, some teach or learn to be junior guides. Callings are as varied in the Spirit realm as they are on earth. I wanted to know what my calling was in the Spirit realm. I saw myself working with energy. I was actually receiving negative energy from earth, transmuting it to white light and returning it back to earth. I also received energy in the form of prayers and sent back comforting energy. I cannot think of a more beautiful way to help.

Pre-Life Planning

When we are ready for our next incarnation on earth, we start the planning. Pre-life planning is the setting up of spiritual contracts and pivotal moments for our next life's learnings. Plans are made for who we will be, which parents we will be born to, where we will live, who we will marry, who our children will be and what things we will experience to learn the things that can only be learned in human form. It is probably the most important information we obtain during a between-life regression.

These plans are not made lightly and start after visiting the akashic records. They are always made with the help of our Spirit guides and our soul group based on our understanding of all our past lives and our current level of progress as Spirit. They are not made with judgment, but with a great deal of love and consideration. The Spirit realm is a place of only love; it is where we learn the true essence of love. We always have our free will in making these decisions, but we often seek the wisdom of those helping us. There is a lot more detail on pre-life planning in the next chapter.

Council of Elders

Once our plans are made, our guide takes us to visit the council of elders. The elders are a group of highly advanced souls or ascended masters who review our past lives and our plans for the next one. They ask us questions and offer loving advice, again without judgement. They then give us a few choices on how we are best able to carry out our plans. Sometimes we can be shown two or more possible lives, with scenes on how planned events might unfold to help us with our goals and contracts.

During my training, I experienced a between-life soul regression. During the time when I met the council, they brought in the soul of my deceased father. Now I only saw him as energy, but there was also an energy passing between us in colours of blue, green and gold. It was a beautiful energy, and I realized this symbolized asking for and receiving forgiveness passing between us. He asked forgiveness for the mistakes he felt he made as a father, and I asked forgiveness for being the rebellious teenager that I was. It was freely given and accepted. Afterwards he asked me to make sure my mother was taken care of now that she was alone.

Understanding why we chose the lives we are currently living helps us understand our circumstances, the issues and struggles we encounter, the family we chose and opportunities or lack thereof that we have. This is not to say that everything is destiny, but many of the major life events were planned before we came to earth. We do have our free will, so it is up to us as to whether we carry out our plans or not. There are also contingency plans set up in case we are not on the right path.

Some people have asked me how we can be sure we are carrying out our pre-life plans, when we lose memory of those plans when we pass through the veil of forgetfulness. I tell them it's easy now. Just have a between-life regression.

CHAPTER 8

Pre-Life Planning and Spiritual Contracts

> Ultimately, then, the purpose of every life challenge is the same; to grant us the opportunity to embrace that which we have so far resisted.
> —Robert Schwartz

I AM SURE THAT YOU have experienced challenges in your life. And at some point during one of those challenges, you probably questioned, "Why me," or "What did I do to deserve this?"

Is it possible that you planned these challenges before you were born? Why would you do that? Why would you inflict this pain and suffering upon yourself?

Why We Plan Challenges

I wouldn't say I was born into a dysfunctional family but one that did not share a great deal of love. I know I chose to be born into my family for two reasons. My father, now deceased, is a member of my soul group. I know of two past lives that we shared. One was in Russia, where he was my older brother and a rebel against the czar. I was about 14 when I went up into the forest behind my house. When I came back, the czar's soldiers had come to my home and killed my family. That was a rough one. The next lifetime we were together was during World War II. We were great friends and soldiers together. My father survived the war; I didn't.

55

But I came back into that same life of his a few years later as his daughter. Members of the same soul group often share many lives together in different roles. The second reason I chose to be born into this unloving family was to give me the humility required to do this work.

Challenges can be planned to help balance karma. Karma as discussed earlier is not a punishment but rather a learning and understanding that helps us progress as souls. We also plan challenges for healing, as a service to others or to help heal false beliefs. Sometimes we make plans to experience contrast or learning through opposites; we learn about joy by knowing sadness or learn about courage by experiencing fear.

Life sometimes gives us our greatest gifts, cleverly disguised as our worst nightmare. There is no such thing as random or meaningless suffering in our lives. Experiencing pain is one of our learning mechanisms. Times of pain and sorrow have the potential for great understanding, to create the opportunity for awareness and to wake us up spiritually. When we set up these challenges while still in Spirit, we also enlist the help from the people and the means that will help us overcome them.

Several years after I was divorced, I was curious as to why my ex-husband and I had the problems we had. I had already forgiven him for his part in the breakup, so I no longer felt bitterness or blame. During a regression, I found out that he was a member of my soul group, and we set up a contract to help me balance some of my karma. We were living in France during the 18th or 19th century and were great friends, both of us male. I was a magistrate in the town where we lived. My friend, who was the same soul as my ex, had committed a crime of some significance and came to me to help him out. I cleared him of suspicion and let the guilt fall upon an innocent man. Now being in a position of trust, I obviously transgressed in letting an innocent man suffer the consequences, which created karma. To balance part of this transgression, I wanted to understand on a deeper level what it would be like to put my trust in someone and have it be completely disregarded, which is what happened in my marriage. It also helped me realize that once the contract was complete, it was no longer necessary to remain married. My ex obviously had his own karma to work out in this or some other lifetime. And I had other karma to work on between myself and the innocent man.

Understanding this contract that we had set up before we incarnated helped me understand the concept of pre-life planning. It also helped me understand some other things about myself in this life, such as the intense reactions I have to movies when I see someone being treated unjustly. I have learned the repercussions of breaking confidences that I have made and that challenges are about how we handle them and not about blame.

It's important to note here that as I give examples of my experiences or those of other people, they may seem overly simplistic. What I can't seem to put into mere words are the emotions felt as we experience these sessions. Also impossible to explain is the claircognizant (clear-knowing) way that these karmic lessons make sense as things start to click into place and you begin to understand how or why it all worked out. It's kind of like having an a-ha moment, but so much more profound. You know it's right, you feel it's right and you understand it on a much deeper soul level than you can ever explain it. As more than one person mentioned to me after listening to their recording, "I feel like I got so much more out of my session than was on that recording."

I have worked with many people who received clear understandings of the challenges they had planned previous to their incarnations during a regression. One woman who came to me for a between-life regression wanted to know why her son had died when he was just a child. Why did she have to experience that? To me, this would be one of the hardest challenges for any parent to experience.

I am so often humbled and overwhelmed by the challenges people have gone through when they come for a session. I never know what to expect. I depend on my intuition and the fact that I am only the facilitator during the between-life regressions. Once someone crosses over into the Spirit realm, their guides, knowing what is best for them and their highest good, take over.

While experiencing her most significant past life, she had lost people she loved dearly and was not able to cope afterwards. When she experienced transitioning from that life into the Spirit world, her deceased son appeared to her as her Spirit guide. He explained that they agreed upon a contract before she incarnated into this life. She would be the mother and he would incarnate as her son. He would be born with severe health problems, be physically ill for all his life and die at a young age.

He explained to her that the trouble she had letting people go in the past life she just experienced was a pattern developed over several lifetimes. She didn't believe they would ever be together again. Their contract was to help her understand that lives on earth are only temporary. That he and other loved ones would always be with her, in past lives, future lives and as Spirit between lives. His coming into life as a physically handicapped individual is a beautiful example of someone choosing a life simply to be of service to others. This regression was beautiful, and I felt incredibly blessed to be part of this intimate reunion between mother and deceased son.

On another occasion, I received a phone call from a woman who had suffered a tragedy in her life. She had heard me speak at a local metaphysical shop earlier that year and took notes while she was there. Later that same week, there was a tragic murder in her family. The person who committed the crime went to see her immediately afterwards and confessed what he had done. She told me that the things I had talked about, along with much trauma counselling helped her get through that terrible ordeal. Again, the importance of this work sank deep into my being, and I felt truly humbled to have been able to help in some small way.

She requested a between-life regression to gain some understanding. While experiencing a past life she found out that soul who was the guilty family member was caught in a karmic loop. As she crossed over into Spirit world, there were many spirits there to meet her. She felt so happy to be there with them, feeling like she was at home and lost any feeling of loneliness. They let her know how proud they were of her for how she dealt with and overcame this challenge. They told her that she was an old soul and one of their leaders. She saw herself in the planning stage of that tragedy. When they asked for a volunteer to try to stop this from happening in this life, she raised her hand, saying, "I'll do it, send me." Although she wasn't able to stop the murder from occurring, her guide told her she was able to make a difference so that he will never make these choices again. She was also told that all karma between them has been resolved.

Seeing this was empowering for her; she could have easily let herself become a victim, not understanding why this tragedy had happened. Her guides went on to tell her that the ordeal was over and her mother was in a place of healing. She had handled the tragedy beautifully, and now she could move on with her life. Her guide spoke to her about some of the talents she brought to earth, and that now she was free to start developing them. Receiving this knowledge from her guides and soul group was a life-changing experience for her.

After any great challenge, people can become victims—depressed, resentful or even vengeful. Dwelling in these emotions will continually lower their vibration. Their ability to make correct decisions will become increasingly harder, and their personal condition will worsen if they cannot heal from the difficult situation.

The more we understand about pre-life planning—that we actually plan these challenges for our own progress or for that of a loved one—the easier it will be to endure and recover from the pain and evolve spiritually. We do not incarnate on earth to have an easy life. The growth we experience from the challenges is what helps us progress as humans and as Spirit. It is why we incarnate.

One young man asked his guides if he still had a lot of spiritual contracts to complete during his current life. They told him he did. Later in the conversation, they told him he needed to have more fun and find joy. He asked how he could do that when he still had contracts to complete. They told him that he did not have to be so serious all the time, and that finding joy was actually one of his contracts.

A friend met her soul group during a regression and found someone there that she hated, someone who had caused her family very much pain during this, her current life. She couldn't understand why this other woman would be in her soul group. Over time, she came to realize that this was a pre-life agreement to help her learn forgiveness. Did the forgiveness come easy? No, it did not, but it did come. It was much better for my friend to learn this concept rather than to go through life hating a member of her soul group.

This is a concept that can be hard to understand. As with my ex-husband, a member of our soul group may actually volunteer to take a negative role in our life or inflict pain, if it will act as a catalyst to help us to learn what we need in order to progress. When we realize this, we can stop blaming the person who we feel has wronged us. This leads to forgiveness; and when we can forgive, we can heal by ridding ourselves of negative energy.

But, once healed, can we go one step further and actually be grateful to that person so no new karma will be created? Is there someone in your life who has caused you much pain? If you can think about this person and his or her actions objectively, is it possible you have learned something from this person? Something that has caused you to grow spiritually.

Throughout all this planning, and while we are here on earth, we still always have our free will. The daughter of a friend had severe drug addictions. This led to her having her children taken away and considerable suffering by everyone involved. During her regression, the woman's guides told her that while still in Spirit her daughter's guides had counselled her that she was taking on too much. However, she felt that she could handle all the challenges she had planned.

While we are in Spirit and still in the existence of pure love, it is easy to forget how we lose our eternal perspective and how hard life as humans can be after we come through the veil of forgetfulness. It is my understanding that if we have chosen a difficult life plan, we may also plan options to exit the earth plane early should we use our free agency to go against the plan.

When our soul enters our physical body, clarity of our magnificence as Spirit begins to disappear. As humans, we start to believe that we are our body. We experience baser frequencies such as fear, anger and intolerance. We start to forget that we are a soul having a human experience. It is comforting to know that there is no failure. We are given the opportunity to try again in the next life, or as many lives as it takes. There is no judgment by our guides, only unconditional love. When we are on our correct path, or on purpose, our guides will work together with us to make the things happen that need to happen to accomplish what we came to earth to do. Some call this luck or coincidence.

After writing this chapter, my daughter's five-week-old daughter died of SIDS. As I mentioned previously, this experience is one of the worst any parent should have to endure, and unfortunately, I now have first-hand experience. Watching my daughter and her husband suffer through this terrible ordeal was one of the hardest and saddest things I have ever lived through. What has made it easier for me is the knowledge I have gained from doing this work. I know that we will be united with this sweet, beautiful soul again. Her sweet Spirit has made her presence known to us in many ways after passing, offering comfort to her bereaving parents and me. I know that this was a spiritual contract set up between her and her parents before they incarnated into this life. When she is ready and not grieving as much, my daughter will have a between-life regression to find out what the purpose of that contract was.

There are days that are quiet; they give you rest.
There are days that are busy; they give you purpose.
There are days that are happy and days that are sad, so you know the difference.
—We Are Many, We Are Us

CHAPTER 9

Soul Groups, Soul Evolution, Soul Mates and Twin Flames

'Our souls already know each other, don't they?'
he whispered. 'It's our bodies that are new.'
—Karen Ross

NEW SOULS ARE CREATED FROM existing energy by our Creator. As new souls, they are taken care of in a type of soul nursery. When the infant souls are ready to leave the nursery, they join a soul group which becomes like a spiritual family. Much study and learning needs to happen before they can even begin to plan incarnating on earth.

Soul Groups

Soul groups have guides and attend classes with master teachers. When it is time to incarnate, the soul groups often make extensive plans and strategies together. They decide to incarnate together in different roles and relationships to help each other accomplish the things needed to learn to progress as a soul. They will incarnate with this group as partners, close friends and family over the course of many lifetimes. In their group they also discuss and compare past lives, what might have worked better and then make soul contracts for the next incarnation to overcome challenges and balance karma. There are many other soul groups that become secondary people during their lifetimes.

Soul Evolution

A soul group generally leaves the nursery and progresses or evolves at the same time, and therefore has the same core soul colour. New souls are white, and as they start to mature their energy or frequency increases and their colour starts to change to a pink and pinkish red. With more learning and growing, frequency colour changes from orange to yellow and green. More mature souls will turn blue to deep blue and an old soul will be purple to gold. Of course, there are all different variations or combinations of these colours within each group. Soul colours sometimes have halo colours that surround the soul. Halo colours reflect attitudes or beliefs attained during incarnations and will change more often than the core colour. These soul colours should not be confused with human auras.

Soul groups evolve, or grow in consciousness, in stages as the colours above indicate, by learning and having callings while in Spirit as well as incarnating on earth together. Relatively new spirits just starting to incarnate on earth tend to focus on survival. They may have a lack of earthly moral principles and are often found in rural locations or may be a member of primitive tribe or extremist group. As souls start to mature and the soul colour changes to red and orange, they find safety in structure and order. They have firm beliefs in right or wrong with no in between and suffer extreme guilt if they don't abide by the rules. They find security living in orthodox communities, such as Amish or Mennonites.

Young, or yellow to green, souls come to earth and develop worldly ambition. They may want to do good in the world but are driven by ego and are attracted to fame, fortune and power. Think of politicians, actors and those rising up the corporate ladder. It is believed that this stage represents the highest percentage of people on earth today.

As humans, a blue or mature soul is more reflective and empathic, less egocentric. They do a lot of soul searching, looking for the deeper meaning of things. Values change from me to we, and they often become healers and lightworkers. Old, purple to gold souls, incarnate with a sense of inner peace and unity consciousness. They usually detach from social conformities, living in the world but not of the world. They can often be found teaching things of a compassionate spiritual nature.

Each of these stages of soul evolution may consist of hundreds of lives and thousands of earthly years.

Soul Mates

Often, people, mostly women, want to know if or when they will meet their soulmate. Or sadly, they are already married and feel they have just met their soulmate and want to know if they will ever have a chance to be together. Many have the unrealistic expectation of the Hollywood version of a romantic partner, one that completes them on every level. Someone who understands their every unspoken desire and is always there when they need them.

In a soul group, there are usually two souls that often, but not always, incarnate together as lovers. If a spiritual contract is set up between the two that they will meet, then they will almost certainly meet. Synchronicities are created that will guide or trigger certain thoughts or actions during their lives to make this happen. But what one must consider is what are the terms of the contract. True soulmates will want to help each other grow and evolve spiritually. This may involve situations like learning forgiveness, bringing an end to unhealthy patterns or balancing karma. That does not mean the relationship does not include a beautiful loving relationship, but you may not recognize your soulmate because he or she does not fit that perfect version you may have created in your mind. And although we tend to think of a soulmate as a romantic partner, he or she may also come into our lives as a friend or family member.

So how do you know if your partner is your soulmate? You will feel it in your heart. Trust how your heart feels, not what your brain or the Internet tells you. Meeting a soulmate often sparks immediate attraction and instant connection, a feeling that you have known each other forever, because you have. The relationship is intense because the depth of the connection is not just on a physical level but also mental, emotional and spiritual.

Twin Flames

I have heard many different explanations as to what a twin flame is, especially on the Internet. There are quizzes that will let you know if you have met your twin flame by just answering a few multiple-choice questions, or articles giving 10 signs that will let you know you are twin flames.

I have had young couples come to me hoping to find out if they were twin flames. Most of the time they are soulmates. To explain what a twin flame is, you must remember that there is always a part of a soul that stays in the Spirit world; this is the higher self. At times a soul may decide to split into more than just two beings—one human and one Spirit. Depending on how advanced the soul is and the reason for incarnating at the same time, the soul could split three or possibly more times, so that they can have two distinct lives on earth simultaneously or overlapping by several years. This is what a twin flame is; two fractals of the same soul on earth at the same time. Souls that come in as twin flames are usually advanced, looking for accelerated learning or a higher cause.

It is not that common that twin flames meet in their shared lifetime, but I have worked with a few people who have met their twin. This is how I came to understand the correct meaning of the term. Often when someone is experiencing a past life, I will ask if he or she recognizes someone from that person's current life. I have explained this fully in the chapter 4. They are not recognizing the body or the relationship but the soul of the other person.

While regressing a woman to a past life, she remembered herself as a male blacksmith. His wife, whom he loved very much, was ill, so he bought a necklace to take to her. While they were together, I ask him to look into her eyes (the window to the soul) to see if his wife was someone from her current life. As the blacksmith she replied, "I don't understand. It's like I'm looking into my own eyes."

I didn't understand either, so we decided to ask her Spirit guides when she connected with them afterwards. They explained that she was, indeed, looking into her own soul. In the life as a blacksmith, his wife was a twin flame. As an old soul, this client has shared other lives with her twin flame, including her current life. During this lifetime, they married young and had a daughter. But the marriage only lasted a year or two because they just couldn't live together. Their relationship was too intense, they were too much alike. However, more than 40 years later they remain best friends.

Another woman was told by her Spirit guide that her twin flame, who was also female, appeared in a past life as her gay partner, which was forbidden in the time period she had regressed to. But there was a soul contract set up so that her partner could help heal her. In their current life they found each other again and became immediate friends and then partners. This time they met so that she could provide the healing for her partner. This is a beautiful example of accelerated healing and learning.

A young girl who didn't seem to have a lot of self-confidence came for a regression. This girl loved her mother so much, she thought her mother was the most amazing person in the world. In fact, it was her mother that gifted her the regression. In the past lives she explored, she had stopped herself from being happy, because every time she was happy something happened to change it. When she was connected to her Spirit guides, they told her she lacked confidence because she felt she was undeserving of love. After her guides gave her a healing to help her overcome her lack of self-confidence, they told her that her mother, who she thought was so wonderful, was her twin flame. They told her, "Love yourself the way you love your mother, because you and your mother are one."

I love soul lessons like this. Our Spirit guides are so much wiser than we are!

Think of your soul group, soul mate and twin flame like a soul family. Choosing to incarnate on earth is never easy. We leave the knowledge of our soul family and a realm of unconditional love to join a human body. We know we are going to experience hardships we do not have as Spirit: pain, sadness, fear, loss. Clarity of our life as pure Spirit disappears. We start to believe we are our human bodies and listen to our ego. Isn't it comforting to know we have chosen to come here with those spirits who are our family? Those who want what is best for us and empower us. Those who would only hurt us if it is to learn a lesson and evolve spiritually.

There is one other situation I learned about just recently that I believe fits into this chapter. Earlier I said that no one I worked with has reincarnated as someone famous. There was, however, an instance where someone regressed to a past life as Jesus. This was during a group regression, where I cannot venture into individual work. I didn't not believe this person, but I also didn't understand it. So, I hesitated mentioning it. While this book was being edited, this person came for a personal regression. Once again, she regressed to the life of Jesus, which was a fascinating lifetime. When she connected to her guides, an archangel appeared. He explained that the Spirit of Jesus was an extremely advanced Spirit, and that after his earthly life many fractals split from him. He explained it as Jesus is the ocean, and the fractals are drops of the ocean water. Understanding this, we can determine that it is possible for more than one person to regress back to the same lifetime.

SECTION 4

Otherworldly Learnings

CHAPTER 10

Other Times

I would rather have a mind opened by wonder than
one closed by belief.

—Gerry Spence

I ASK YOU TO KEEP an open mind while reading this chapter.
If you had asked me 20 years ago if I would have believed
everything in this chapter, I may not have. But after working with
the people whose experiences I am sharing, and understanding
their sincerity while they are experiencing, I believe them. I don't
know how I could not. I let them know that I am not here to judge,
and that no matter where their regression takes them, it would be
pretty hard to shock me.

A few things to note: I am careful not to lead people during a
regression. I do not work with people who are mentally unstable.
These types of regressions are much more common than you
may want to believe and come from people in all walks of life.
Dr Michael Newton has said that it is impossible for people to lie
while they are experiencing the altered state of hypnosis.

For clarification throughout most of the chapter, I have used block
quotes when the messages are exact words from clients or Spirit
guides.

These examples are the memories of the past lives of my clients.
If there is any conflict with your beliefs or your understanding of
these places, I leave it up to you to believe what you wish. I offer

these examples as proof of the incredible calibre of the souls on earth today. This is a time when many souls have volunteered to be on earth to help raise the vibration of a world in crisis.

Atlantis

Many people I have regressed have gone to past lives on Atlantis. Many of the women were priestesses or temple workers. Although I have personally never regressed to a lifetime on Atlantis myself, two women saw me working in the temples alongside them. I have never asked to explore a lifetime there but would love to in the future. Life on Atlantis was described as very spiritual in the temples, as well as extremely advanced scientifically outside the temples.

During one regression, my client experienced the collapse or sinking of Atlantis from an apparent earthquake. He has very kindly shared his account of what he remembered of that lifetime.

> I am a male, middle-aged, white, human, educated. I am overseeing a group from an observation mezzanine, and they are intently working on an experiment. I am in a discussion with another male and female in the room. I believe this to be my superior and his assistant of sorts. I am being persuaded to try something on the experiment that I do not want to do. The meeting seems contentious and is going on in an adjacent area to the work area. [I am] Overlooking others working at tables

or lab benches, control panels of sort. I see a female intently working on something. A decree like a presidential order, giving us the go ahead to conduct this experiment or exercise. Uniforms are a grey rayon-like fabric, silky but not natural.

The man in the room is very tall with blond or grey hair, an authority figure directing the experiment. I have the feeling that he is not doing the right thing. I am a director of energy or operations, something like that. I have a team of super-smart individuals. We are working on a large power unit that is like a reactor, a frequency reactor. (At the time we regress I am having a hard time understanding what we are doing. I got the sense later that it was time-space frequency power experiments, trying to turn back time.) We have run many experiments. I am warning them not to run the experiment that way. My team is not in favour of running it. I am told that we must as this is necessary, but we don't realize the repercussions and a chain reaction may occur. An unstable condition exists. I am angry as I am powerless and must submit to the hierarchy. I lack courage and will be disciplined. They operate from fear-based control.

I go home. There is not the hustle and bustle I expected. I believe I walk and carry a bag, and my kids rush to the door to greet me. I bend down and embrace them both, and my tensions melt away momentarily. My wife kisses me and asks about work, and she can tell I am having a rough time. Our home is condo-like with stone, steel and lots of open windows. Sandstone and light grey in colour, but lots of intricate stonework. A simple design, low in structure in my case but many buildings are tall. My home is comfy but a little sparse by today's standards, and the lighting is just there. The rooms are lit, they kind of just glow. Furniture is like form-fitting. We sit down for dinner, and it's a small portion of tasty vegetables. Our custom is to hold hands and pray, but not many do this. I get the sense that spiritualism is not popular at this time.

God is a concept, but we are much more science focused and push to achieve technological achievements. Spiritual meditation and flow are concepts I have learned, but do not apply outside of home for fear of repercussions.

I am back at the laboratory. Technicians are panicking, people running around. The experiment is out of control and there is a feeling that we can bring things back into control. But it's worse than we suspect, and the system is overloading. Authoritative Nazi-like figures are in control. I am trying to keep a calm mind and analyse the problem. The earth shakes and no one is really in charge as things get worse. [Was this] time shifting en masse? My group is in favour of halting operations until we figure out what caused the seismic activity. [The ones in charge] do it anyway. They up the power and it temporarily works and then the whole works explodes, and that destroys the vast majority of our civilization; buildings crumbled and the land dissolved and

sank. I see this as I ascend. I watch; I feel I'm
meant to. As I return in Spirit there are smiles
and tears. My wife is there; she knew this would
happen. A premonition maybe. A shame; it was a
beautiful life, and it's all gone.

In that lifetime on Atlantis, this client felt he could not convey his
opinions enough during the meetings and backed down because
of the hierarchy of scientists. He related this to his career in his
current life, where he works with a type of electrical energy.
Understanding the lifetime in Atlantis gave him the courage to
stand up for what he believes in with his current life career.

Lemuria

A woman came to me and wanted to understand why her husband
was always wanting her to be tall and thin, which she felt caused
her to overeat. Her regression took her back to a lifetime in
Lemuria. She offered a fascinating description of what her life
was like there, which I am leaving in her own words as much as
possible. She had very little, if any, knowledge of Lemuria before
this.

She found herself on a mountaintop with a flat shelf on top. It was
not a pyramid but a place she would go to meditate and look over
the land. There were stairs inside the mountain and a doorway to
the flat shelf.

I come here to think; I have to make a decision.
There is a danger for my people but we don't

know what it is. I get impressions in my head, it's
wisdom we can tap into, it's telepathic. It helps us
make decisions. There are only a few people who
can do this.

She was very tall and thin and wore sacred robes. She was female,
not a priestess, but sat on the high council. She felt Lemuria was
a matriarchal society. I asked if the soul of her current husband
was there.

He is a lot younger than I am; he aspires to be on
the council to get training. I am 34, but time is
different. He is 27. He has an amazing mind. He
has to pass the tests to be able to communicate
and to tap into the wisdom. You have to learn how
to control it and open it. We do not marry here, but
we have partners. We have a good relationship.
Sometimes we live together, but I have my own
place. I organize. I have no children. Some people
have children, but we are the council consisting of
three women and two men.

Lemurians ... our history is that we are
part human and part celestial. We're a hybrid.
Celestials couldn't take the atmosphere, so they
had to create hybrids who could handle the oxygen
and nitrogen. Their's is another galaxy. There are
three civilizations here [on earth] Lemuria, Asia
and Africa. There is no other human incarnation
before us.

There are artisans, teachers, scholars. It's
a communal life. It's a very healthy society, no
pollution, mainly vegetarian and fish eaters. Very
spiritual. Everyone has their input, and we all

work for the common goal. Peaceful. There is very little crime, and if there is, they are rehabilitated.

Going forward to a major event in that lifetime, she saw ships with huge white sails coming into the harbour from surrounding islands.

There is a threat to the safety of the people; we don't know what it is, but we are aware that it's coming. We have to find places for them to stay, make sure there is enough food and make sure they are not diseased. I have to organize this. There are shockwaves, like soundwaves being felt. I can almost see them. They are like rings of sound ... shockwaves. They go out as far as the islands. People are afraid. It's technology we don't understand. We don't know how to stop it.

We have distant neighbours. They are much more scientific. They are doing very amazing work, we know this, but we also know there is a threat.

I asked if she felt the distant neighbours was the continent of Atlantis.

We don't call it that. They're harnessing the sun's energy through the crystals, but they haven't got control. I agree that it's going to be an amazing energy source, but they don't know how to control it. The shockwaves are getting really intense. They have weapons. They are using crystals for weapons as well. They are fracturing ... fracturing the earth.

I asked if she would be on the council her entire life.

> No, I can step down from the council to retire, and do more studying.
>
> I have been on the council a long time, I am 74. We age slowly. At 74 here, I would be like 45. There was so much responsibility. There have been a lot of changes. More people have come. The shockwaves have stopped for a while, but [the distant neighbours] are trying different things.
>
> I don't like some of the decisions being made. I think [the council] are making a big mistake. I'm an empath; that's why I can feel so strongly what is going to happen.
>
> They don't understand what's going to happen. I don't know why, because they are all tapping into the same information that I am. It all points to the same thing: major chaos and upheaval.

I asked if the upheaval happened during her lifetime and then took her forward to that time.

> They have no idea of the power they have. The ones working with that huge crystal, it's very powerful. No, no, no. There are huge tidal waves. Storms, a lot of people die. It's the end of Lemuria as we knew it. Some escaped; they got to higher ground in the mountains. They live there where it's safe. I stayed to help when the tidal waves came. It was my time to go anyway.

When she connected to her Spirit guides, she asked what she had learned in Lemuria that she could apply to her current life.

They are telling me it's not my fault. I have to forgive myself for not having the power to not change their minds. I was only one of five. I couldn't have stopped the destruction no matter what I did. I can stop feeling guilty. I only needed to understand that life. I don't have all the responsibility in this life. My biggest lesson from that life was having to make the decisions, and trying to live with the decisions.

My husband should stop making me feeling guilty. It's not my fault. He has no recollection of his life there, but I do. I know his place there and my place there. I think he holds me responsible unconsciously. Regarding losing weight, it's something I do have control over. I can enjoy eating, I just have to be careful; diabetes is just down the road. I need to start exercising. My guide said my husband doesn't care what I look like; he will always love me.

I asked if she was an empath in this life. She replied,

Once you are an empath, you are always an empath.

"Nice," I replied.

Yeah, until you are an empath! But now I only pick up individuals, not whole continents. It helps me understand people.

Extraterrestrial Interpreter

One woman found herself as a priestess in ancient Egypt. She had contact with celestial beings or extraterrestrials who communicated with her telepathically. She acted as the interpreter for the Pharaohs. There was an agreement that the Pharaohs would not hurt other people, and in return the celestial beings would give them information on technology to help them evolve. Another woman I regressed also lived in the time of ancient Egypt. She received information from celestial beings through sound vibrations.

CHAPTER 11

Other Worlds

After the earth dies, some 5 billion years from
now, after it's burned to a crisp, or even swallowed
by the Sun, there will be other worlds and stars
and galaxies coming into being - and they will
know nothing of a place once called Earth.

—Carl Sagan

Planet of Creation

DURING MY TRAINING, I REGRESSED a woman who found
herself in Spirit form on a planet of creation. She was there as a
student with other students, all in Spirit form. She was learning
how to create a flower. Now this may seem like a fun and easy
thing to do, but she explained how she had to make sure it would
only affect the flora and fauna that already existed on the planet
it was intended for in a positive way. I often look at flowers, trees
or insects now and wonder what was going through the minds of
the people or spirits who created them.

Lives as Pure Spirit

A few people have found themselves without bodies, in the form
of energy or pure Spirit. They are simply existing, floating in the
heavens. They do not seem to identify with a home base. However,
they are able to be wherever they want by thought process, simply
thinking of where they want to be. This is not the same as crossing
over, where they are met by their guides. I believe it could be in

a mental plane, where some spirits go to rest after a particularly hard physical life.

Mars

About eight years ago, two different people on separate occasions found themselves on the red planet (Mars). The planet was near destruction (death) in one case and already destroyed in the other. When near destruction, the people went underground to live. Both clients expressed a love for this planet, and both were sad over its destruction. Isn't it fascinating that NASA recently sent the rover Perseverance to Mars to look for signs of past life?

Shortly after this, people asked to be regressed to life on other planets, other worlds or planes of existence as one of the past lives they wanted to explore. This has now become a common request, and people often find themselves on other worlds.

Creator of Worlds

There are some regressions that affect me deeply on a spiritual level. They seem to stay with me forever. Some of the souls that come to me are just so advanced that it astounds me. A man in his mid-40s came to see me. He used to be a life of the party type of guy. But, he had been in a terrible car accident the year before. He was unable to work because of injuries he had not completely recovered from. He was depressed and only found joy in being with his young daughter.

As he stepped through the tunnel, he found himself floating as pure Spirit. It felt so freeing because without a body, there was no pain. He was filled with love. There were other Spirits there that felt like family. They were observing the galaxies and how they work. They just seemed to be existing and observing. I asked if there was a teacher or leader. He said there is a golden light and became very emotional. It was the Creator.

He asked the Creator why he had to suffer so much. The Creator replied, "Please, son, be strong; this is part of your journey. This physical life will end soon and you will return. You came to earth to experience having a body and the pain, suffering and darkness that goes along with it to understand that creation is not just happiness."

He was told he only needed one life on earth, and he had the accident to understand this in a big way. He needed to know loneliness and all the hardships of earth life before he could return. Previously he had been having thoughts of suicide. He was told he must stay longer to ensure the lesson in one lifetime, and that it would give him a glimpse of his true reality.

In that life as Spirit, he was learning how to create. He then went forward to when he could watch the evolution of the creation of a planet.

> It starts with a spark, then crust builds and builds until it reaches full size, next comes the atmosphere. (There were a few steps I could not understand.) Then water and plant life.

All during his regression he just kept expressing what he was seeing with words, like wow, incredible, amazing. And sometimes his voice would just trail off as he watched this creation unfolding. I had trouble understanding everything he said but was hesitant to interrupt and ask him to repeat it. I have to remember that it is more important for the clients to experience than for me to understand exactly what they are experiencing.

He was so amazed with the love he felt that went into planet creation. I asked if planets were always round.

Yes. Every planet must rotate.

He went forward to a time when he started to create planets himself. He could take a spark from a sun to start the creation. I asked if he put life on the planet.

The planet is life.

I asked if he populated the planet with humans or other beings.

That was another group of spirits. But the creation of souls and spirits must be created to replenish the planets.

New planets bring more light into the darkness of space. Where the planets and stars end, new planets and stars are created as an expansion of light, life and love. So this group of spirits will keep continuing to create new planets. There is no limit to the expansion. There are galaxies beyond galaxies as the universe becomes a multiverse. These planets will have life on them. The more life the more love, and the less darkness.

I asked about earth.

Earth is just a small spec in the scheme of all things. Earth is a dark planet, and its purpose is

for souls to come here to understand the darkness
of duality (pain, hate, etc.).

At one point in the middle of speaking he just stopped and said:
"Wow! I just saw a supernova."

The planet had just reached the end of its life, but it was comforting
because God was always watching.

Every planet must have a cycle, must be renewed
if it becomes too dark.

He came to earth so he could understand this darkness, that
some planets must have an end so that darkness cannot overtake
the planet. He came so he could understand that every planet is
fragile, and as he created planets, he must always add a cycle of
destruction to each one.

He was able to observe different galaxies and was able to
travel between them quickly through thought process. He left
understanding his true being, with a sense of renewed purpose
for his current life. I gained a new understanding of the planets
and the universe.

Abductions

I have worked with people who have been abducted or are
continually contacted by extraterrestrials. This affects people
in different ways. Some need to find missing time periods, hours
or a whole day that they cannot account for to find out they were
abducted. Others have sworn me to secrecy before they came for
a session, as they do not want anyone to know this about them
for fear of being thought mentally incompetent. How sad that

someone can be more afraid of humans than the extraterrestrials that visit them regularly. And still others are writing books about their own experiences, so I will leave it to them to tell their own story. In some cases, people can find themselves on the ships and have memories of seeing extraterrestrials on the ship. But they have little knowledge or memory of what happened to them while they were on the ship. I believe this could be because they did not know what happened to them, or they were blocking the memory because they did not want to know.

Pleiadean

I have a Pleiadean connection, and what I like to think of as a galactic family. This has been revealed to me personally, by several channelled sources. I have asked for a name for the purpose of communication, which is telepathic during meditation. At first, they would not give me a name because they said that would cause separation. Then they referred to themselves as We Are Many, We Are Us so that I would understand I was part of them. Later this was shortened to We Are. I asked what life was like on Pleiades, but they didn't want to tell me so I would not become homesick. I asked if I would return to Pleiadean life after this incarnation and was given the following answer.

> It's not a place you return to, it's a place you are continually part of. It's not separate places or separate planes, it's integrated all at the same time. It is all part of everything together, simultaneously. At this particular time your greater consciousness is on Earth.

Future Lives

There is also a future-life projection, where you can experience a future lifetime. This would give credence to the fact that all lifetimes are happening at the same time. I would never take someone forward in their current life. If I took them to a certain time and they were no longer alive, it could be traumatic.

I experienced a future life where I found myself high on a plateau. I was a teacher, teaching about six young children. We had light bodies that shined like white light with a very light-blue tint. All communication was telepathic. I received information from the ethers and passed it on to the children. One small child named Elius then stood at the edge of the plateau and communicated the information to the people below. I remember seeing the information leaving him as though they were radio waves. I have no recollection as to what the information was about. This future projection was experienced during my training. It was a group projection, so we had to move on when the teacher told us to. Group regressions or projections are a great way to understand if you can remember past or future lives successfully, but the lives cannot be delved into as deeply as during a one-on-one session.

Starseeds

If you have been on social media at all, you have probably come across terms such as Starseeds, ascension, the new earth or the age of Aquarius. There is enough information on this for a whole other book, but I will give a brief explanation here.

Starseeds are souls who have incarnated on earth, often for the first time. Not young souls, but interplanetary souls who are highly evolved. Their home base is on another planet or star system,

Pleiades, Arcturus and Sirius being very common. Pleiadeans are us, from the future, here to assist us with the ascension process. Starseeds have volunteered to come to earth to help raise the vibration or shift the consciousness of the human species to help us ascend into another dimension, out of the 3D world through the 4D and into the fifth dimension. This dimensional shift will happen when humans become more spiritually advanced and are ready to live in unity consciousness. Our DNA is changing to adjust to these new frequencies and changing humans from a carbon-based being to a more crystalline-based being, which allows us to hold more light. The earth is also increasing its frequencies and vibration and will ascend into a new earth. The Starseeds are being born with their DNA already adjusted to the new frequencies. However, coming through the veil of forgetfulness, as we all do when we incarnate on earth, they can often feel different, out of place or unable to deal with the lower vibrations that still exist on earth. During the altered state of hypnosis, they access their subconscious, which allows them to remember their purpose, and they experience an awakening. They often are or want to become healers or lightworkers. Younger Starseeds are coming in already awakened.

When Starseeds already know they are Starseeds, they ask to regress back to a life on their home base. One Starseed found herself on the planet Sirius in the form of pure energy or Spirit, where she was a Spirit guide. Life there was peaceful, calm and loving. She came to earth to radiate love and light.

Another experienced a past life on a small planet. Her skin was kind of rubbery; she had a large head and only three fingers on each hand. She was an explorer and travelled on a spaceship to find food sources because her planet had exploited all their resources. Their water was drying up. She incarnated on earth to be an energy healer.

One woman lived on a clean and pristine planet that was always light, no differentiation of night and day. They were androgynous. She lived and worked in buildings that looked futuristic. Colours were very light, in shades of pink and purple. She worked on projects that had to do with helping their natural environment. They had very different types of plants. Her people were healthy and calm, not so emotional, and they did not have to eat. They were aware of life on other planets; some visited other planets, but she did not. She chose to be born on earth to help with the ascension process.

Yet another woman found herself in a gathering of beings with a type of physical bodies that are defined by light (light bodies). They were welcoming her back home after an incarnation on earth. Her home base is called Cascade. It is beyond the Milky Way. It's a peaceful and spiritual planet with beautiful crystals that come out of the ground. She incarnates on earth because she likes it here but finds it hard to take on a physical body. Some of the times she came to earth she did not take a human body. She came this time to teach, heal and share experiences. She knows the earth is awakening to a higher consciousness.

I find these regressions fascinating. However, they can be quite unsettling for people who are afraid to talk about their experiences, think they may have been abducted or have not yet awakened to their purpose and don't understand why they feel they don't belong here. If you have any of these feelings, I urge you to get help, whether through regression, energy healing or even researching online. If you feel you have been abducted or think you are a Starseed, please look up Mary Rodwell, who is a leading researcher in the Starseed, UFO and contact phenomenon areas. She can be found on Facebook or online at acern.com.au. Her website has a full list of resources. She also has two books sold on Amazon: *Awakening* and *The New Human*.

Millennial Starseeds may enjoy reading *You're Not Dying, You're Just Waking Up* by Elizabeth April. A Starseed herself, EA has been living in LA for a few years, but is now back in her home province of Ontario. You can also find her online at elizabethapril. com or on her YouTube channel.

CHAPTER 12

Channelling

We will speak with you, because we are you!
—Rheuvane, Member of the Council

THERE ARE MANY DIFFERENT TYPES of channelling. Most of us are intuitive. That still, small voice or gut feeling tells us if we are on the right path. This is a connection to our own higher self. We are the source of the information or guidance.

Mediumship is communication with those who have crossed over. A medium will read the Spirit energy that surrounds a person. They will get actual verbal messages, mental impressions or images that relate to the deceased. Usually people go to a medium when they have lost a loved one and want to know that they are well.

A channel receives messages from higher dimensions, usually a Spirit guide or a collective of higher consciousness. Many people who channel always tap into the same guide(s) or consciousness and refer to them by name. These messages give clarity and support spiritual growth for an individual or for the planet.

There are natural-born channels who have made a pre-life agreement with the collective they will channel as part of their life purpose. We all have the ability to channel, and with practice can receive our own interdimensional messages. If you desire to channel on your own, know that the messages should always be positive, uplifting and comforting. You can find many people who offer channelled messages on the Internet. It is a good idea to use discernment when listening to these messages. Make sure they resonate with you.

Channelled messages are often given as mental impressions, and the channel acts as an interpreter to convey the message in human words. Channelling can also come through as inspiration in the form of art, music and science. There are also deep trance channels who allow a Spirit to enter into their body. They are not aware of what is being said and need to record the messages. In this case I have found that sometimes the Spirits may have trouble finding the right words in human language, because they are used to communicating telepathically or through emotions.

The Council

In my work, I have connected and become good friends with a deep trance channel. She refers to the collective she channels as the Council. They speak to us as 4 or 5 separate entities representing the collective. Her voice changes slightly with each entity. I am the lucky one who gets to speak to her guides directly and ask all the questions. This can often be emotional and overwhelming. Her guides have told me not to be overwhelmed, we had planned this before we came to earth. They have given us much personal guidance.

They have also given us messages that they want us to pass along to everyone willing to listen. Please find these messages below, and know that they are shared with the intent to inform and uplift. If messages seem a bit choppy or repetitive, it is because the messages have come at different times or maybe as answers to questions. I have tried to put them in an order so they may be best understood.

The Council's Definition of Channelling

There is certainly an influence that comes from the sixth and seventh dimensions—a psychic perspective that comes through to help people change their minds. This positive imagery and strong loving energy will descend on you, covering you like a blanket. We are shifting the energy from the negative and destructive. People who take time to meditate, to love, to experience, to especially sit and listen and open themselves up are much quicker to receive or tap into this energy. It's being offered to everyone, but some people in their evolution are able to obtain it more readily. When there is balance you can channel light. But when things are out of balance on earth, you can channel things that are not from light.

Messages from the Council

We will speak with you, because we are you. You are connecting to the collective source. We don't speak in human words; we speak in emotion. We will use human terminology because you are in human form, but you and I and Source are collectively one. When we bring information to earth, when we give you a message or direction there will be clarity, to speak to you in a way you will understand.

As water evaporates and materializes on another planet with a purpose bringing certain information to these places, our bodies wear out and dematerialize, and we return to Source with all our experience and become part of the collective consciousness. We carry with us seeds of emotions from our incarnations on earth.

People were given certain gifts and the ability to individualize. Individualization evolved to a more troublesome place as far as falling away from connectedness. Society has become too individualized, and you have lost many of your innate abilities with each other and your understanding of source. Our connection—we are all part of source—collective consciousness is lost. People used to work in such unity and now they are unattached, involved in rudimentary pleasures and material things.

Our main goal is to open people's soul eyes to see we are a whole. We are all one. We are a whole, but when we come to earth and become individual forms, we take individual paths—my life, my soul, my past life, my car, my house, my job, my guide. But we are of a whole. On the other side of the veil, we are a whole. We are all working towards the same goal—unity consciousness.

We are all of Source. We play different roles at different times in different galaxies. There are other souls from different galaxies on earth now. On earth as a human, you think of yourself as an individual. We are all part of the same. On other incarnations, on other planets and other times you would have varying levels or degrees of individualization. Some planets are more evolved and some are less evolved.

When we are one, we are always evolving. We gather information (light) to feed our love. In order to continue to evolve we need to continue to bring in experiences. It is what we are. By raising the consciousness of each individual, promoting, adding to, enriching every day in every way that you can, by bringing light, joy, love through acts of kindness. Interaction with others, people, plants, animals, everything is energy, treat everything with positive intention.

The amount of damage done to earth in a recent amount of time will take a long time to correct. We need to go back to our roots. Our innate nature has been turned off. We are more interested in our material things than we are about the life for our children. If you are hungry, we feel this. If you are hurt, we feel this. If you are in pain, we feel this. We feel the pain of every little child that is starving. But we have to operate from the big picture in order to bring the earth and your people back to your roots. We understand from the bigger picture. We know that your lives are just a moment in time. Please understand that you have been part of this planning when you were with Source.

Your world is in extreme turmoil. It's all part of what is needed to bring a change in attitude or perception of how the world should work. There will be a oneness. It will ascend on earth. It is ascending more quickly, but will cause some spasms in how people and the earth will adjust. Duality is in the throes of death. It offers a bedlam of issues and energy. In the next short period of time, which will be 25 to 35 years (at the time of writing), there will be resolution. There will be a cleansing—it will come through as a mind cleansing (attitudes), and there will be a gradual change for more love, more peace.

You are at the right place at the right time. What is taking place is what has been agreed upon and planned. If you feel that you are stuck, you are just having some downtime. Stop and smell the roses. As you do that, you evolve as a whole. You will go forward when the time is right. If you are in human form you are on the right path. Just keep all your interactions with love and light.

We should always be working on a global basis, as the collective. There are more people who are evolved and becoming aware of what is the right path. We are winning the battle. There is a plan, and the plan is working.

If you are hurt by someone, or angered by an experience, visualize where it is in your body, why it came and watch it leave your body and go to where it can be absorbed. This can be done through meditation or guided imagery. See what emotions you are feeling in your heart and understand what has put that there. If you hold these hurts or emotions in your body, they can cause illness and sickness. Let go of anything that is not of a light or loving nature.

Be more connected to nature. Mother nature is the tangible manifestation of Source that sends out energy of calm. (I love this!)

Archangel Michael

Clients sometimes channel when they connect to their Spirit guide. Besides getting personal messages, they sometimes receive messages that are beneficial for the rest of humanity as well. The following is an example of a channelling from Archangel Michael. It was unexpected, and more of a question-and-answer session. The questions were not thought of in advance but based on the conversation I had with this client before he was regressed. All personal messages to the client have been removed. The actual questions are included to give context.

As I am speaking to the channel, I (M) am asking the questions to Archangel Michael (AAM) who is responding through the client.

M: Should we study the Bible?

AAM: Of course. Everyone should. You should at least read it— give it that much respect. But you have a tendency to magnify every passage in the Bible. Please keep in mind this is a great book, written about Jesus and his teachings over a very short period of time. He is with us. We are attempting at this time to bring in more energies to be able to reach more people, than God and Jesus, which is a very, very effective method of communication. But for some, it alludes them.

M: What is there more than God and Jesus?

AAM: All other beings that help God and Jesus assist.

M: Like who?

AAM: Like myself.

M: What is your origin?

AAM: I am a consciousness, we are many beings on many planets, solar systems, universes and galaxies.

M: This is not something the Bible teaches.

AAM: This is not something the Bible taught 2,000 years ago to people who had no conscious way to interpret these things. Ten thousand years ago they would have understood. In many ways man has not evolved; they have gone back.

M: What can you tell us about the state of the earth? There seems to be so much dissension.

AAM: Excitement.

M: Good excitement?

AAM: Raising the vibration of the earth.

M: To a much higher level?

AAM: Things will become much more pleasant, but for some it will become intolerable.

M: So there is a divide?

AAM: Yes.

M: Will there be more peace?

AAM: Yes. Only peace.

M: Will there be more contact with otherworldly enlightened beings?

AAM: Yes.

M: Are they here now?

AAM: The have always been.

M: Will they make themselves known?

AAM: They have already done so. It is not a question of if they are ready, it is if you are ready. When you are ready, you will see them.

M: Where are we now?

AAM: We are at a precipice. People have done many, many things in the name of progress, which has actually put mankind, humankind behind. It is our desire that everyone be one with us. There is so much. So much.

M: What is the best way to be one with you?

AAM: You must ascend. You must purify your souls; you must purify your hearts. It is very hard to do that when you continually do not appreciate the life you have been given. There are many selfish intentions of man. We would like there to be much more peace, understanding, compassion. As you can help practice this—we will help.

M: Explain God to me. Is God a consciousness?

AAM: He is the collective consciousness of all beings that were ever created.

M: Of everywhere?

AAM: Yes, in his domain.

M: Are we talking millions and billions?

AAM: You cannot imagine.

M: Do we have the capability of joining this one day?

AAM: Yes, this is our intention, so you can go on and help us create other worlds and other civilizations so they can reach levels of enlightenment.

M: And on and on and on into eternity?

AAM: Yes.

M: And how close are we to becoming, not God, but whatever is next? Spirit?

AAM: Not having to come back to earth anymore, to live in peace. Earth is a beautiful place. But don't become too attached to it. There are many things in this universe; you have a very limited knowledge base in your current life.

M: But we are starting to open up now, and that is why it is so compelling to want to know more and more. And yet sometimes it feels like we can't know more.

AAM: When you give all of yourself 100 per cent of the time to achieve that ascension and consciousness and one with each other and God, that's when you will all be ready. You still have far to go.

M: Do we all have to be there at the same time?

AAM: No. Others are already there.

M: We go as we reach the frequency?

AAM: Yes. Channelling is a frequency. Once you achieve it, you will channel.

M: How do we reach that frequency?

AAM: There are things that are likely holding you back in your life. They hold you to the earth. To old ways of thinking.

M: Can people channel from the wrong sources?

AAM: There are many beings coming in now.

M: Are some malevolent?

AAM: Some.

M: How do we discern good from bad channelling?

AAM: Intention should be clear. Question. Pray.

M: Can they speak partial truths?

AAM: Yes. Do not be afraid. We are here. We are with God. He is here. He is in all of you.

M: We are God?

AAM: We are God. We are one. We will not leave you.

M: You cannot?

AAM: We will not.

M: Can we leave you?

AAM: Yes, that is your choice.

M: Thank you so much for speaking to us today.

AAM: May God's divine energy shine upon you.

Shortly before the final transcript of this book needed to be submitted, Archangel Michael unexpectedly channelled another message through a different person. I asked if I could add it to this book, and he agreed. He said this book was needed and part of my life's work. (Tears welled up at this confirmation.) Note how the message and delivery changes. They are based on the channel and what they wanted to find out during their session. When he says you, he is referring to all humankind. Again, personal information has been omitted so this is just an excerpt of the whole message.

AAM: You are here to experience fun, which brings joy and

happiness and raises your energetic vibration. Anxiety is a low energetic vibration from a human not wanting to evolve because they are attached to their human form. Fear, guilt and shame lower your vibration.

The world is changing, it's going to be different. You don't need government. This isn't what human life is supposed to be like. Not hierarchy and controlling. Humans have the ability to live and love in peace. That's who you are. You are pure love.

This is what you have to understand, this is evolution, and in order for you to evolve and get to the 5D this all has to happen. You're not going to like it. It's going to be messy.

A lot of people are going to want to give up. This is why you have to continuously work on yourself and raise your energetic vibration. Because those that do that will survive this. This was supposed to be an experience, but not one of destruction. The elements are not here to serve the human, they are here to serve something much bigger than that. And if need be, they will do what needs to be done.

You are destroying yourselves and the earth, one of the most important - the earth. But if you do not, the elements will do it. Because it is time to evolve into something more than this game you guys have been playing for so long.

Your only job is to love and to work on your own evolution. You are one, so as you do this, everyone else will evolve. And those who do not will parish. It's time.

M: What about first contact? Will we see signs of other planetary beings?

AAM: They are already here.

M: Will they be known worldwide?

AAM: They are known worldwide. Those that will need to see it right now will see it. But as you block it, they are observing you. When you block it and trust not to believe it, they are not going to show themselves. They come down, they look, they wait. They look to see if you are ready. Too many of you are not ready yet. When you will be ready, it will be normal. You are not ready.

My Favourite Message

I am ending this chapter with my personal favourite message. One that has helped me immensely during difficult times in life.

> When times get hard, look through spiritual eyes.
> When you look through worldly eyes, you focus
> on loss, pain and suffering. But when you look
> through spiritual eyes, you are connected. You
> know that your suffering is only temporary, that
> you will be with deceased loved ones again and
> that we will all return to a realm of peace, joy
> and love.
> —Jenard and Rheuvane, Members of the Council

SECTION 5

Final Note

MY PRAYER

You do not have a soul. *You are a soul.* You have
a body.

—C. S. Lewis

Don't think of death as some tragic ending, but as a way you
planned to return home. We are eternal, timeless beings journeying
across these two worlds—the physical and the spiritual. We are
individualized sparks, fractals of Source, learning and progressing
in both worlds until we return to the collective.

The veil between the physical and spiritual world is thinning at an
incredibly fast rate. The frequencies and vibrations of our bodies
and the earth itself are accelerating consistently. More and more
people are awakening to their divine truth. Those who seek, who
wish to receive more knowledge, more insight, more light will
find it.

Now, during this brief moment of eternity, as we are spirits in
human bodies experiencing life on earth, I hope you will see life
through spiritual eyes and keep an eternal perspective. May you
find all the answers to your questions. There are many ways to do
this; regression is only one of them. But it is the one that helped
me so much. It will help you to remember your divine truth.

It is my prayer that you will find peace, love and joy on this earthly
realm before you return home once again.

EPILOGUE

At the end of writing this book, I had a conversation with a dear friend and mentor who urged me to share my recent experience with my mother. I share this because I was able to have this experience from what I have learned. I also share it because you are also able to connect with deceased loved ones like this during a between-life regression.

As I mentioned earlier, I did not come from a loving, close-knit family. My father owned a store and worked long days, seven days a week. My mother loved us in the way she knew how, but in way that taught me how not to be a mother. Growing up I felt that she was bitter, I know that she was critical.

Mom suffered from dementia and crossed over at 96, just a few months ago as I write this. I spent a week with her a few weeks before she died. Travelling to be with her was difficult because the border was closed due to the Covid 19 pandemic. With her dementia she was in and out of reality and slept a fair bit. She became childlike, and even liked to play tricks on me. How nice to see her true Spirit before the world hardened her.

She had regular visits from her brothers and sisters who had already crossed over telling her to join them, but she could not or would not let go. She had a fear of crossing over. I spent hours with her, telling her what it would be like on the other side. She had lots of questions, which I was able to answer. And the next day, we would repeat it all again.

Mom would come up with lots of excuses as to why she had to stay. One was that she would miss her house. This is a small wartime home that she bought with my dad when I was just six months old. She was adamant that she would not go back into a nursing home. She just wanted to die in her own home, and she did a few weeks later. I told her she could have a big, beautiful house on the other side, any type of house she wanted. She told me she didn't want a big house, just a small house. And she didn't want anyone to visit her who had been mean to her. By this she meant my father and brother, both of whom passed before her.

What a realization this was. I realized that the last six months of her life were some of the only happy times of her life. My niece and nephew had become her 24/7 caregivers and were wonderful to her. They waited on her, prepared her meals and took care of her personal needs with love and affection. No wonder she became the innocent childlike Spirit she truly was.

It was her birthday a few weeks ago. She would have been 97. So during my meditation, I decided to wish her a happy birthday and ask her how she was doing. She came through clearly. She told me all about her little Tudor-style house. It only had one bedroom with a big, beautiful bed and a large living room. There was no kitchen because she never wanted to cook another meal. But she had a coffee maker. She loved to have her coffee out in her garden. The garden was her favourite place. And she could change it every day. She showed me that, by waving her arms like the conductor of an orchestra, she could change the colour and arrangement of all her flowers. She had finally returned home and found peace, as I knew she would.

ABOUT THE AUTHOR

Marilyn Kaufman is a certified hypnotherapist practicing regression therapy in the Niagara Region of Ontario, Canada where she lives with her husband. Regression work has taught her about eternal progression throughout all lifetimes, past, present, future and the in between.

A true believer in life-long learning, Marilyn started her metaphysical journey 25 years ago studying meditation, yoga and energy healing for several years. A spontaneous past life regression changed her course of study to spiritual hypnotherapy. She studied with many of the trail blazers of this work in the United States and Canada. Incorporating past life and between life regression, spirit guide contact and neurolinguistic programming with her energy work, Marilyn offers her clients a unique experience, therapy for the soul.

It is her hope that this book will encourage all who read it to try regression for themselves, and realize that their true nature is really that of a magnificent spirit having a human experience.

For more about Marilyn and her work, visit www.youareasoul.ca. @lifetimes444